PERFORMANCE

James Reaney

«Back from Getting the Mail»

P•O•E•M•S

MOONSTONE PRESS

Cover: James Reaney, *Unsuspected Aviary*
Illustrations: James Reaney
Back cover photo: Susan Reaney
Inside back cover photo: Morris Lamont, © *The London Free Press*

Designed by James Reaney and Lise Gunby
Produced by Gunbyfield Publishing
Printed and bound in Canada by Hignell Printing Ltd.

Moonstone Press gratefully acknowledges the assistance
of the Ontario Arts Council and the Canada Council.

Cataloguing in Publication Data

Reaney, James, 1926-
    Performance poems

Poems.
ISBN 0-920259-32-4

I. Title.

PS8535.E35P4 1990   C811'.54   C90-095060-9
PR9199.3.R43P4 1990

Moonstone Press
P.O. Box 96
Goderich, Ontario
N7A 3Y5

AUTHOR'S PREFACE:
A Letter to the Reader & the Performer

Without knowing I was doing it, on April 5, 1960, at Hart House Theatre, Toronto, I premièred a performance poem called *One-Man Masque* which turned out to be a suite of connected poems interspersed with prose vignettes and meant to be recited or acted within a circle of symbolic props, half of which stood for the experience of Life and the other half for that of Death. I used a rattle and a recorder; as I went from babyhood to old age, there were bits and pieces of costuming; once I reached the world of death, I donned dark glasses and furry gloves to put a baby doll into a coffin, or was it a baby carriage? There was a barrel into whose hollow depths I recited a poem about a ghost.

I shall never forget the thrill of having a reaction of 400 people at a time to my spoken voice, almost as many as had bought my first volume of poems. Immediately I wanted to further all this by experimenting some more with adjustments to rhythm and images. So, later on, I moved into choral poetry for big groups of people. There is nothing more exciting than hearing twelve voices belting out a Donnelly chorus; the effect of the quieter, lonelier lyric with its rhythm of meditation is like a wild bird's nest half hidden by grass — ahead lies a large pond dancing with waves and whitecaps in the wind. Both are wonderful.

And so, in this volume, I have brought together performance poems written since *One-Man Masque*. They can be read silently, they can be read aloud, they can be scored for many voices along with all sorts of illustration and commentary from mime, dance, musique concrète, manipulation of props and body movement. In whatever way you wish, try out these new pieces as a way of giving groups of people an experience of poetry's power to reach out and focus an audience that may have long forgotten how nursery rhymes and street games stir up the soul with the joy of unifying so many of the senses, so many of your friend-circle.

Not all of the poems are finished, but challenge you to expand their patterns into larger works with your own local reference. On request, the publishers will supply you with suggestions for performances as well as lists of composers and other experts who may live close enough to you to help you get things going. Performamus!

James Reaney
June 1990

ACTOR'S FOREWORD

"Performance Poetry" is one of those expressions that scare the hell out of folks. Kind of like "Modern Dance" or "Video Art." Images of oddly dressed people chanting, moving in disconnected ways — repetitive video patterns flushing meaning at us. We end up shifting our butts in our seats and stifling yawns. But this need not be. Often these forms are mis-understood by us because they are misused by the practitioners.

Why is this? In the case of "Performance Poetry" (in reality, just a free-form of theatre) many of us have been damned by bad teaching of poetry in our schools. Fuzzy Yates, my Grade 9 teacher, waddling down the aisle, eyes closed, mumbling "Tyger, Tyger, burning bright" through sucked Pep-O-Mint. Guaranteed to lose thirty-one teenagers. Imagine if she'd pushed back the chairs; got us to sing "In the jungle, the mighty jungle, the Lion sleeps tonight"; then from there a quick leap to the creation of Blake's tiger's world — a cacophony of sounds — turn that waste basket upside down — make sounds — make of it a tribal drum — speak into it for organic echo — run chalk along the board to recreate a frightened animal's screech — feel the goose bumps that sound raises — imagine the jungle's fear of the tiger. Create the fearful symmetry of that world. Feel the poetry; perform it. We'd hear the poetry then, I'll bet you; and hearing is what it's about.

When I first worked in a James Reaney play, *Listen to the Wind*, we had twelve chairs as props and set. Those chairs become trees, laneways, houses, beds, horses, whatever. It was the first time I'd done *that* kind of theatre. It was also the first time I realized that we could use words, poetry, the same way we used those chairs. We could do anything with them. That's what "Performance Poetry" is: building a set, an environment, a world with those words. A good poet writing about the wind can make you hear the wind. Try making the sound of the wind itself under those words. Underline — draw out the world of the poetry. Perform it.

David Ferry
April 1990

CONTENTS

◆

JANUARY:
ETHOS

For this collection's format, I have adopted something much looser than the conflicting gyres of life and death chosen for *One-Man Masque*; I've grouped the poems and prose-poems into a calendar. There is no underlying story, except possibly one I may not have discovered yet. It occurs to me that fragments of the book may fit together into variety shows, mental landscapes, whole evenings. As you see, in several sections there are backbones for larger poems you can write and perform yourselves with your own personal and local material. One thing: I love southwestern Ontario very much — that's a possible plot, and I also could live in word and storyland forever, and hope to.

Also, I would like to add here a brief commentary on January's order and contents, called "Ethos" because I wanted this section, as is this month, with its Twelfth Night & other parties, to be filled with people, and people, says Aristotle, make ethical choices that determine their characters over and above what their genes and their environment choose for them. In the "Actor's Foreward," we hear from a favourite actor of mine who played key roles in *The Donnellys* with superb flair. This is because when the poem, *November: Images of War and Peace*, was published, Armistice Day, 1989, I happened to show it to David Ferry and Jerry Franken and their wives, Kyra Harper and Dorothy Chamberlain, who immediately gave it a performance première in a farm-house kitchen at the Little Lakes, Stratford, with styro-foam cups and other pick-up objects. David and Jerry have worked with me in countless workshops with big and little people, so they both should have a "say" in this book which owes a lot to their expertise and also to their willingness to join a movement which, at one time, seemed outlandish and even infantile.

Domicile is the first poem because, on the first day of the year, the two poets in my family, here called Janus and Janna, the doorway god and goddess of houses in Republican Rome, welcome the reader to a house with twelve rooms in north London — it used to be called Broughdale.

Next we meet a refugee from an unfinished suite of mine called *Collegiate Olympus*, in which the poet sees his high-school teachers as the twelve Greek gods — whose statues sit around a little-known backyard of the Acropolis as if at a tea party in an unroofed teacher's room. This poem about Miss McDouglas is based upon the myth of Venus arising from the foam of the Cyprian Sea when the testicles of Saturn fell there, having recently been cut off by his sons — Hades, Poseidon, and Zeus — in protest at his exploitation of their mother's fertility. Here, I suppose, I see Miss McDouglas as the Venus of our Souwesto Mediterranean world where, as Peter Moens once remarked, "There is so little touching of each other that they all go to chiropractors, these Ontario Puritans, to actually feel someone hugging and crushing them and stretching them!" Could this great English teacher goddess have resulted from the dumping of a box of Sunday School cards into the sea from some Presbyterian minister's trouser pockets? Read on!

The Lament of the Poet is based on Sir Charles Goddam Roberts and Wilson Macdonald and W. O. Mitchell and myself, who have all of us read at Lord Roberts School — a pedagogic challenge. I really admire the old bastard's (Goddam's) pre-Laytonic sexuality. By the way, a great Russian poet, I heard him, asked the ladies at a reception if any of them were willing to go to bed, now that the reading was over. This frank overture was met with indifference. A member of our History Department reminded him, "Yuri, Canadian girls usually like to get to know you a bit beforehand." Like six years? I think the League of Canadian Poets should consider the moral and emotional problems here. After all, ancient rhapsodes must have had some sort of release-after-the-reading escape valve.

Imprecations was first performed at Mingles — in the old City Hotel at Dundas & Talbot, where the Donnellys had their London stage stop. My wife and self have given this poem at least six performances, perhaps most notably at Harbourfront in 1985. Check Souwesto audiences for those likely to be riled at swear words; *i.e.*, this poem does not go over with The English Speakers' Union.

And January ends with a poem commissioned five years ago by the CBC State of the Arts programme which had recently taken over from Bob Weaver's established Anthology. They asked for a satire on our literary and cultural scene in a *vers de societé* montage of a fictional literary party. Zena Cherry, who, for years, had written a widely read society gossip column for *The Globe and Mail*, was now retired and I set out to imitate the rather dotty grandeur of her style. The commission was generous and this enabled me to hire my son and daughter-in-law to help me think up cultural guerillas who should be invited to the party, as well as absurd rhymes for their often grotesque names. Along with other sound effects, the CBC added, at the very end, the sound of a Canadian blizzard merrily roaring away as the guests became snowbound, and sleepbound, stuck forever at the gateway to Time's next encampment.

I mailed a copy of the script to Zena Cherry, who telephoned to tell me she was sorry to have missed "such an interesting party".

DOMICILE

Janitor & Janitress are we
Of this verandahed domesticity,
Itself a place of lightning rods
And kitchen gods.

There are doors and wind eyes,
Weeping drains & chimneys.
Outside on Huron Street's cement,
Through summer heat & winter sleet,
With their pedestrian feet,
passersby make daily comment.

From night walkers, tipsy commotion
Of Western scholars we pray
For protection.
Our doormats stolen, neighbours say.

Visitors are welcome,
But should obey our superstition
That IT'S UNLUCKY to come in one door,
Leave by another.

When we die, please, please
Take us out feet first
      Lest
From our new home,
Whether in graveyard
Or funeral urn - - - - - - - - - - - - - - - - - -
- - - - - - - - - - - - - - - - - - we - - return!

«Ancestors»

MISS MARY McDOUGLAS

Miss Mary McDouglas was a teacher of mine,
(antibacchic amphibrach paeonic iamb);
Stratford Collegiate Vocational Institute,
(trochee amphibrach paeonic dactyl);
Bred from those who were Pictish Covenanter
Long before John Knox the Ranter
Chopped off the head of Mary the Mermaid.
Scores of young men on their wedding nights
Tried vainly to escape (Miss Mc's) metrical analysis
Of their first-time ever activities and, trochaically,
        Went down to defeat
        With a female iamb.

With glee from my own private modest inferno,
I used to imagine her from this planet ejected
Through light years of space till dead she fell,
Scottish-canuck comet
Onto just a young unsuspecting planet
With no mountains yet, no land in sight,
Just an even six-mile-deep sheath of water,
Archaic, pure, sterile,
Virginal, puerile,
Spinning around an inexperienced young Mazda,
        This pearl.

The mix of Miss Mary McDouglas's corpse
Fermenting in this innocent clean eyeball
Was Volcano Presto! extrusive storms, Permian beer,
Jurassic nightmares, Pleistocene mammothry,
And peaceful sheep, giant ones, twenty feet high:
These must have been descended from her hair,
White, rigidly, smoothly marcelled that day
For the At Home Dance that night where the Principal
Danced with her . . . "I beg your pardon, Miss McDouglas
        This line's metre?
Is, I think, highly irregular, line nineteen, you say?
        Amphimacer?

THE LAMENT OF THE POET

After announcing the title, there is a silence, then:
In that year, had I the appointment in Creative Writing
From Dr. Rhodenizer at Acadia,
Yes, whose family is mentioned in *Sam Slick*.
Since he was lame, they put him to college,
Instead of the lumber camps.

I was young then and had — most of my teeth.

For writing 20,000 lines on St. Catherine Tekakwitha,
I was given, in 1922, free board at a seminary.

Did it never cross your minds
That you're all in a book I'm writing?
If you'd feed me better
Why, your farms wouldn't be so rocky.

These are uncoloured, sell for 75 cents.
If hand-coloured, a dollar.

Most of them are signed.
If you prefer, I have some unsigned ones.
Oh God in Heaven, that pig of a critic
Who had the gall to say
That it was hard to find a copy of my poems
Not spoiled by my autograph!

Somewhere, in the swamps of Southwestern Ontario
I gave a reading once to bumpkins
In a rural building with a tin roof.
The moment I opened my mouth
To read my elegy on Percy Shelley
In which I compare him to the drainage system
Of my beloved Tantramar marshes, then, guess what:
It began to rain, raindrops like hungry woodpeckers.
No one could hear my voice.

In 1935 I was knighted. "Sir," you must call me,/And, Evelyn,
when I marry you, you will be called/"My lady." Still, my
comb is all but toothless,/Even my clothes brush is missing/
.... too many bristles.

11

Unfit for a doctoral thesis, said Dr. Mabel Brickbank
To a loyal student fan. Unfit, my beautiful poems,
When every pair of tight blue jeans in this confederacy
Receives five $ a lb., from the University of Texas's
Manuscript collection for his or her
Foul papers, & any other Dead Sea Scrolls at hand
Such as laundry lists & used toilet papers!

Last night I received a phone call
To come read at Lord Roberts School.
At twilight, I reconnoitre the schoolyard of my enemies.
Note well. *Nota bene*. It is carpeted with large pebbles
Suitable for throwing at a once-famous poet.
Over the prairies, see that eagle flying high
"along that pathless coast —/The desert & illimitable air —"

With a tortoise in his claws.
Eagle! As you did with the bald poet Aeschylus,
Drop it on my skull, put me out of my misery. No?
No, no, no, no. No. Must I go on/, then?
"Just a half an hour more, sir. The school buses are late."

When, deserting my wife & children,
I ran away to Greenwich Village,
My eldest boy shot himself.
            I had to come back for his funeral.
              Oh! anything to drag me back.
Charles, however did you learn the trick
Of twisting my bowels? From your mother,
            No doubt, no doubt.

Out in Saskatoon, after my reading at the Humanities Club,
I remember till my dying day, the look on their faces
When I asked them if they knew of a place
Where I could get a woman for the night.
Perchance, some pretty young thing
            sitting right here in the hall
              Might . . . ?

You see me as rusty, angular with rimless and black ribbon.
You should have seen me at the Salon for the Manipulation
Of soft tissues, not far from the intersection of Spadina
And Queen. After the tea, after my reading at the Kirk
Of Predestination, King Street, where they fired a young minister
For daring to say that a loving God could never
Have made the cruelties of Hell. Let no hellfire go out!
Otherwise, we shan't be able to control *them*!

Yes, I too have been known to grab the Barley Wet Nurse,
And give her savage suck till winter is over,
The studio couch has grown to my back, I swear, rise
To put on my overshoes — go down to the Public Library.

Oh, shut up! Tell me where I found you, Evelyn, in a shack
With 500 Carnation milk tins! Just before I die,
I swear I shall marry you. You'll be a noble dame yet!

This young man they have hired, Earle Birney, to edit CPM
Instead of me!
And this whippersnapper who dares to write on my topic —
The sinking of the *Titanic*. I shall show you,
I'm doing my own version of the sinking of the *Titanic*
From the viewpoint of the Iceberg. Poor iceberg.
No one thinks of how much a puma suffers eating
Mangy cows. I am that puma. I am that iceberg.
My dear, we're due at the King Cole Room in ten minutes,
Mustn't fail to put in our daily appearance.
The only salon in Toronto, myself with you, Elsie,
And Myrrha, all thinking I might marry one of you.
Do none of the professors *ever* come in for a drink?
Making $ out of teaching me, they won't buy me a drink.
Quite a stiff walk from Summerhill,
And, of course, we can't afford cabs. To be asked —
To resign the editorship of a fourth-rate cage
For mouldy nightingales. But — survive. It balances —
I SEEK MY MEAT FROM GOD!
Aye, and, to be honest with you, He doles it out
Now a rat, sometimes a groundhog, no venison anymore.
If the tortoise the eagle dropped had hit me, surely —

Even my death would a, somewhat, have sent up my sales?

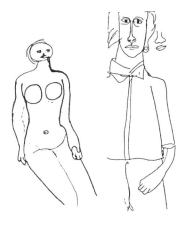

13

IMPRECATIONS
The Art of Swearing

Sunlight breeds moon- and earthshine, movies and candles,
But volcano light comes from the depths of our mother.

You tell me that cursing is become a lost skill?
That men would rather you physically hit and kill?
Though a timid Sunday School gold star attender at heart,
Perhaps I, a non-swearer, can revive the art.
Then we can teach it at Western: Swearing 22.

My own father never swore except — 'you dirty beggar!'
Never *bugger*. *Beggar* — as damn becomes darn, and God
Is always Golly where the bright angel feet
Of Elwy Yost have trod,
But my stepfather was quite another story:
'Great Judas Iscariot — that fart in a windstorm!
Get off my toes, you bloody cocksucker!' — to a horse.
'Son of a sea-cook' was his mildest imprecation.
On a daily basis *shit-ass* and *piss-willie*
Were levelled at neighbours, relatives, those
Who deserved this, those who did not.

There was a story he'd tell about the livery stable
Up town behind Harrison's Beauty Parlour on Erie Street.
New owner didn't know people yet,
Asked Marty Halpin, an Irishman,
When he came in to sit by the stove with the others,
'Mr. Halpin, do you know Mr. Robertson here?'
Did he know Mr. Robertson? They were deadly enemies.
Their farms adjoined, they'd uprooted each other's fence-
posts so often, they never ploughed in contiguous fields,
But sent out their hired men instead. So Halpin said:
'Yes, I've met the son of a bitch before.'

And — when young Liisa got a bad review from our local critic,
she said: 'May he be tied to a stake, and die in the flames
Of his own critiques which I will pile up, all his reviews
Around him.'
Helped with these local traditions,
I have set myself to try my hand at cursing.

14

———◆———

Here on my bed upstairs I lie in my double-breasted suit.
I am filled with ink.
I sharpen my pencil with the penknife they gave me.
May parents gave it to me last year
Who before this year is out will be divorced.
Their one body which is I
Will then be torn apart
In court   unless
I refuse to take off my clothes
Which now hold me together,
Paper over the cracks.
So I fall asleep in my clothes
And dream . . .

1

A curse on the man who invented Westminster Sherry.
      $1.25 a bottle, the worst in the world,
Mysteriously brewed in a county without one vineyard,
      May you, sir, be boiled alive
            In the urine of the 400 old tramps
      Who under the bridges suck your zinc breasts tonight.

In our heads they say there is a city.
The tears of rage I weep now were once its fountain.
You two who leave me like an unfinished sculpture
My tears could pursue you as an angry river.
But instead they
Up to the sky
And freeze to cirrus clouds filled with sundogs
      Pulling heavy clouds stuffed with snow —
Which now falls down on the golden tropical town.

2

A curse on those oil workers who in Alaska
On their condom weekends hired helicopters
To hunt down grizzly bears; a curse on those
Oil workers in Arabia who on their Sheik weekends
Had nothing better to do with their jeeps
But run the last Arabian ostriches and gazelles
To extinction. You I tie to these burning sands,
I the djinn of the ostrich, the gazelle's angry angel,
Sprinkling grain over you I summon Elijah's ravens
Who fed him but rend you.

The Independent Grocers' Association wants to build
    A shopping Plaza across the road
      From the Temple of the Children of Peace
        In the village of Sharon.
May you swallow a penny and pass a pound.
May a young infuriated Jesus Christ
Beat you all the way to Parry Sound.

The tramp and his trull, my mother and father,
Trudge through the rain.
If by nightfall they are not out of my kingdom
They will be dragged back and drowned in my tears.

Three Curses by Tall Women —
A Queen St. whore, Edith Sitwell, Judith Donnelly

At college I used to walk every street and lane of Toronto.
    One evening came upon a crowd
      Of short cabdriver men around a tall woman
        Her stockings rolled down to just beneath her knees,
Fresh from the beerparlour, looking for customers,
Tall broad woman, she turned on her suitors
    And cried:
'Wipe your face on my arse'.

I, Edith Sitwell, was an electric eel in a pond of catfish.
    I was also a giantess who was much derided.
    Never should have left my father's park.
Surely there were some gazelles who refused to leave the ark?
    But you know I did, I did want
      Someone
        To come
I desired the embrace of a fellow giant.
The men I did love hated women.
For not daring my boma of thorns, letting me die in sleep,
    I call you cowards, dwarves, midgets,
      Men!

The night after they changed the inscription over her tomb
to read *died* instead of *killed*
Mrs. Donnelly said: 'So the new priest
Has changed the inscription over my tomb
to read *died* instead of *killed*, has he?
As if we were victims of Madame La Grippe or of Senora
Influenza,
Or of a strange, strange mass heart attack.

There's this new theory of the French that disease
Is caused by a tiny invisible thing — a bacillus.
May the bacillus that caused my death also, priest,
Approach your gentle and headachy ecclesiastical
Skull.
It was a bacillus shaped like a pick axe,
Pick-axe from ear to priestly ear!'

Rain till it runs into a silver city.
   Thunder I deal from my pack of weeks
      Into a brazen town, into an iron town.

And now, some last minute curses on the lighter side.

a) Oh ye hippies and merry draft dodgers who in the sixties
Came to University College stampeding my dear old professors,
Mobbing them till they scrapped the old Honours English Course,
And gave you the anything at any time:
No down payment of Emily Brontë, Virginia Woolf now,
Beowulf later on, a literary cafeteria for
Academic piggies. Communitas delenda est!
May you in Heaven be presented with harps tuned in this order:
A 2 octaves below Middle C, next F natural 5 octaves above High C,
Next . . . and may your conductor Saint Cecilia shout:
Saint Saens' *The Swan* by sight or OUT!
Having failed the harp test, may you fall into Hell
Where the only pitcher of water
Stands at the top of a staircase whose steps
Can only be climbed in the following manner:
Step #102 first, then step #3, then step 52, then 7 . . .
Yes, in precisely that order, you mental grasshopper,
      Or no water!

b) Poetry is optional, says Betty Education.
Oh Great Betty, when the rebirth vats
Are wheeled out and you ask for a new body,
May the Great Partmaker in the Garden of Adonis
Say as you ask, 'What about an eye, got any eyes?'
      'Eyes, Betty, Ears, Betty? Big toes, Betty?
         We don't stock them anymore.
There's not the demand there once was.
   We've run out.
         They're optional.'
Optional optional optional

c) And to the inventor of those deadly foes of poetry
            The *Dick, Jane and Puff* readers,
May the prose of your marriage remain
Two simple short declarative sentences
In a frowsty motel room, two sentences separated
            Forever
By a tough period, a full stop, and no co-ordinating
Conjunctions available at counter
Downstairs or under it.

And last of all, you Archbishop of Banality,
      You bookmoth, you committee worm,
Endlessly prolonging a poet's torment
      At interminable English Department and League of Poetry
Meetings,
            May God in Limbo
                  Table your motion forever.

Thunder I deal from my pack of weeks
            To a rusty town, drought I think
            And the once golden city
Has become a mud town, slaveway expressed,
            Pushbutton Acres.
As my curses and spells worked, their God became
            The Priest who shrivelled into a Burgomaster
            Into a Mob.
So with these curses is a wheel formed for a chariot
            That drives through the flood of bitter ink
                  Flowing from the divided boy long ago.

Liisa, I wonder when we get him tied to the stake
            And pile his reviews around him
Do you suppose they can catch fire?
And yes, Mr. Halpin, the more I find out about Robertson —
The Servant Girl thrown down in the yard squirming
In the dust with the 2 boys on top of her:
'Yes. I know him, yes —
I've met the son of a bitch!'

THE PARTY OF THE YEAR

Zena Cherry, eat your heart out!
Right now I'm at a party
Which, if you had been a smarty,
You'd have written in the *Globe* about.

There's hockey players, wrestlers, athletes, and movie stars.
There's slick rock bands with computerized guitars.
There's all the winners of the awards known as Junos,
Most of whose names — who remembers or who knows.
There's modern composers who know not flats and sharps.
There's traditional poets with antiquated harps,
And drama critics, plump, vampiric and sadist,
Looking for the stray and unsuspecting dramatist,
Critics on the prowl for hints of post-modernism,
Writers viewing this with not much enthusiasm.
Ouzounian, Phillips, Wood, and John Neville,
All dressed in shades various of crimson and pink —
Why they've come in disguise as bottles of red ink;
Provincial premiers, blurb writers, grantsmanship experts,
Various kinds of cultural hacks, all kinds of stuffed shirts —
Zena, Zena, you who wrote in one of our most worthy newspapers,
Admit this cultural soirée outdoes your Rosedale capers.
So here I am, a shy reporter
Drifting about with tape recorder
At the party of the year
About which you more will hear,
How with mirth and jollity
They decorate the tree.
Out! you Simpsons' Department Store windowdressers,
For of our noble tree you would be morbid messers,
Trying to hang upon its branches human limbs dissected,
Not at all what Eaton's would have recommended.
Instead let's make paper chains from *United Church Observers*.
To string this green macaroni we'll ask the conceptual art performers.
Who's this gliding thro' the crowd?
'Tis the well-known New York singer, Mary O'Dowd.
With special training from Arthur Eggleton
She's going to sing all of O Canada over a megaphone.
With golden baseball bat, climb! Mary O'Dowd to the top of the tree.
We're prepared to listen to you in somewhat anxious ecstasy.
Why what is this I see
But Arctic triumph for the N.D.P.
It's the socialist Yukon contingent
With their plump new premier, Tony Pennikett.
Instead of frankincense and myrrh,
They bring recently skinned Conservative fur.

19

Kicked out by our neighbours for *Sea of Slaughter*,
Here's Farley Mowat with a large female sea otter
And hundreds of baby seals adorable,
Safe at last from Newfie slaughter so horrible.
How dare you suggest there are too many hordes of them.
These blue-eyed infant seals are sweeter than cherubim.

Athletes now up from the basement wend,
Some beerbellied, hulking, other more slend-
Er; e.g., Mario Lemieux of Penguins #66.
Bring your Oiler friend #99 and we will fix
These popcorn bells while André, the Giant,
Makes the Xmas cookie dough more pliant.

Here comes, with sad tinsel, Robert Weaver dressed in black.
Will they ever bring his Anthology back?
Guess what I heard in the cloakroom from one of us:
"This new programme — State of the Arts — is too damn frivolous."
Just a moment, there's Margaret Langerich with her American Cousin,
And David Suzuki, Shelley and David Peterson,
Richard Bennett of B.C.,
And P.E.I.'s premier, Jim Lee,
Not to be confused with Hawaiian guitarist, Al McPhee.
There's Michael J. Fox of *Back to the Future*,
and Sondra Gotlieb, our Washington voyeur.
Before she gave to our ambassador her hand
A book she wrote, we understand,
About eating her way across Canada:
Breaded veal, coq au vin, seal flipper, raw tundra,
Surf and turf, bear paw soup, and other such culinary conundra.
Actor with the power of fifty tanks
Maury Chaykin lately played Hal Banks.
No, no, we've got one on the tree already,
For gate-crashers please keep your baseball bat steady.
Bob White, United Automobile Workers President,
Subject of a wow TV show recent,
Written, produced, directed by Collison,
Kramer, oh hail they cinema verité — Gunnarson!
Here comes the new Alberta Premier, Don Getty,
Striding over the snows like a handsome Yeti.
And here comes Ed Mirvish with the Queen Mother —
Who was up in the CN Tower this summer;
a Minister of the Environment disguised as a toxic blob,
And now Paul Cowan pursued by a senatorial mob
Who want to throw him and his film to the flames
For saying that Billy Bishop may not have shot down 72 planes,
Down from the skies each flown by a fanatic German baron.
Will they not settle for sixty-nine? seventy? seventy-one?

Up to the door rolls Suzanne Blais-Grenier's golden coach;
In a classy limo Robby Metras does as well approach.
Watch Megan Follows turn her tables:
Can play at hockey or — at Anne of Green Gables.
All's quiet on the Richard Hatfield front, I hear,
But leave that suitcase in the woodshed at the rear.
Conscripted, suddenly, to serve some drinks at the bar,
I mix Ken Mitchell a Bethune rib-clipper.
For David Young who writes plays about Anne Murray and Jerry Lee Lewis,
A special called: "We dare you to sue us."
Loganberry juice neat for Earle Birney,
Just published more poems, though himself nearing ninety.
Blueberry juice for the Rhino Party so *élite*.
Oft did they meet at a bar known as Les Foufonnes Electriques,
Called by them their national hindquarters.
Alas disbanded, no more drink there, their supporters.
Bred in the Bone, how stately some authors o'er their sherry bow;
Joshua, however, by the punch-bowl teeters *Then and Now*.
As I pump beer, I overhear a remark somewhat bitter:
"I don't need a martini every day from Erika Ritter;
So much more my cup of tea
In the afternoons was CBC
With *Mostly Music* and *R.S.V.P.*"
Jeanne Sauvé, Your Excellency, admit,
This is better than the Shamrock Summit,
Where, rejecting your viceregal gold,
They left you callously in the cold.
Here's Ms Margaret Atwood
Who on lecture podium hath stood
At the University of Alabama
Where with great stamina
And deliverance hypnotic
she has lectured on Southern Ontario Gothic.
Mel Hurtig,
Are you still hurting
From years of encyclopedia gestation?
to my secret edification,
The largest picture in your three volumes is not John A. Macdonald,
But that of a glacier. Oh well, we are a nation cold.
Conversations about the summer go like this: "Those summer days —
When constant news of Ronnie's colon kept us in a daze,
As well as week after week of Mulroney's Tunagate
Which certainly made us appreciate
The starving millions' much preferable empty-bellied state."
In serape, Michel Tremblay
Brings in the cast of his latest play.
The old girls order empty glasses to cry in,
And howl, "When will we ever finish dying?"

◆

Season's Greetings to Allan Stratton;
Never mind that Conlogue on your new play sat on
Calling it commercial
Why so at one time were *Comedy of Errors* and Sheridan's *Rehearsal.*

Robertson Davies, if only you'd told us sooner you were raised in Renfrew.
We always thought you were brought up in a Mayfair West-End Mew.
My golly, says someone, was that the sound of crashing Corinthian pillars,
Just down the road to the west of us, Gee Whillikers!
Barbara McDougall comes scurrying in. It's her we thank.
She must have just knocked over another Western bank.
A sudden silence fills the house, as to whose cause I have no clue,
Until — Brian and Mila, so glad you could here ski.
Why you're not one bit like a Kennedy!
Put Daniel Nicholas Dimitri
In the cradle at the bottom of the tree.

Arriving just after the prime minister,
Murmuring Mahler *Totenlieder,*
Here comes milkmaid Maureen Forrester
Leading the Canada Cow
Who is much, much thinner now,
With duller horns, more plaintive moo,
Though still able to support a ballet dancer or two.
Marcel Masse I'm told came in one day
Took away some of her hay,
Turned down the thermostat on cultural notables,
Then disappeared in a cloud of R.C.M.P. constables.
Well, *there* — he's back and leading in the publishing houses:
The Honorable Miss Prentice Hall, Dames Double Day, McGraw-Ryerson, in
gold blouses,
Big strapping branch plant girls
With textbook smiles and computerized curls
Followed by the native, but lesser, dross:
Breakwater and Black Moss,
Longspoon and Queenston House,
Tree Frog and Pargurian.

At last! Here comes the band!
Than Rush much more demonic,
This one's post-punk — even semiotic,
And do they turn up their synthesizer,
Specially designed for them by Murray Schaefer,
Whose latest piece you'll know —
Written for 12 porcupines and a sweat-drenched piano!

Enter Paulette Jiles like Jesse James in the saddle.
Some human ears strung around her neck and the Governor General's Medal.

Lord! how the poets pour in: Mrs. Buckaway, George McWhirter,
Brian Fawcett in a turtle-neck sweater,
Bill Bissett in basket-ball footwear,
And now strides in young Chris Dewdney, bard of geology
Dressed as a trilobite fossil in Ordovician reach for my rhyming dictionary.
His wife is disguised as a pretty cephalopod,
Their new baby Tristan, teething on a brachiopod.

News comes that the Blue Jays cannot attend.
They're with their families in South Bend,
Indiana, Texas, Georgia, California, Dominica.
Ah, we understand, fellas, but — we miss ya.
And on the dance floor it's the tango of biographer and biographee.
Elspeth Cameron, you elegant wasp, and Irving Layton see-saw, saw-see.
When he howls that she has grossly misportrayed him
Sweetly she reminds that he asked her to write it
Roars he: "Beastly have you lampooned me in this life of me."
Roars he and purrs she. Purrs she and roars he.
Loud blows the controversial gale
Still the lawyers and the publishers are happy
For every anguished roar rings up a sale.

Gate Crashers. Rumours of free trade have made certain foreigners
Unafraid to try to drag off Miss Prentice Hall.
She of the textbook smile and the computerized curl.
But Writers Union President is not alone,
For Murry Chakan and André, the Giant, support Matt Cohen
As he hurls those hulking yanks Gulf and Western back in defeat
They soon before this brave, feisty bouncer sneak off in retreat
Though thrown-back curses intimate that they may later come
For the Honorable Miss Prentice Hall with an alligator.

O Marcel Masse, O Maureen Forrester, O Canada Cow, what now?
Well just now the snow is piling up
All beverages have been drunk to the last cup.
The fires are banked, the candles gutter
The north wind rattles at every shutter.
After front doors and back doors locking,
We all hang up a sock or a stocking.
Snowbound, who can roam?
There's no use in going home,
And so the party falls asleep,
While outside bombardiers roam through the snow so deep.

Zena, Zena Cherry, eat your heart out!
I've just been to a party
Which, if you'd been a smarty,
You'd have written in the *Globe* about.

23

FEBRUARY:
DIANOIA

The chap I call my speaker, or persona, has ideas, when he's not suffering from the other kind of noia — paranoia. *The Granary* sees a father as a woman with a snake between her legs; the *Greenland* poems see language as a huge bird that talks to us; *Serinette* was written for the installation of John Beckwith as the first occupant of the Chair of Canadian Music at the University of Toronto. The idea is obvious that, like Mussorgsky with *Boris Godunov*, we ought to be able to field our own operas: *Oh Alan Dayton* presents the experience of being painted — Colleen too, from photographs taken in the back-yard; *The City of Secret Proportions* owes a lot to James Anderson, Perth County archivist, who stood one whole night on the court-house roof to protest City and County Councils' lethargy re our historic past; just as dawn broke and the police arrived, James heard the pigs mentioned in the poem.

«Rural Dandy»

THE GRANARY

You stand in the door of the granary.
Horses' heads bunting below in stalls.
You look out at the snow.
Behind you cobwebs, dry darkness, bins
Of ancient & curiously differing seeds
Each of whose advents changed lives.
Caused armies to march, towers to be built,
Empires and kingdoms to rise and fall:
Powerful vowels in the human printing press.

BARLEY — with his beard, his awn, king of taverns.
BUCKWHEAT — swarthy, Saracen prism, afternoon farmers' crop.
OATS — feathered, financial, northern, survival saga.
WHEAT — cloven, empereur, dolly, imperial, enemy of hunters.
ALL — building houses in Chicago, fortunes in Odessa, Power.

THROUGH ALGAE PAWS FROM THE SEA long ago came these PERSONS.

My head become my hands holding them.
I saw them larger now as beckoning kings.

PLANT US, they commanded.
The winters are long in your father's dark bins.

Outside in the doorway the seasons whirled by,
Moon with half her face torn off,
Now white, now green, now black,
Sun rising at Anderson's then at Haiden's, then at Otto's farm.

A SMALL BEARDED BLACK SNAKEWOMAN my father
Grew larger and larger behind me, hands on my shoulders.
The trick, he said, is *when* to sow them.

Through the open doorway I saw rain, sun, a page of crows,
Heron equations, a whirlwind of soft snow.

NOW! he said. NOW!

◆

THREE GREENLAND POEMS

1. A Lake in Greenland

My dear, there were lakes in Greenland,
A lake in Greenland where
Gentle as wishes on ideas
The rain fell as it falls here now.
And in that Greenland there then flew
Butterflies large as books
Birds who did not need to sing
Their feathers so glittering and knew
No other winds but those that blew
Southern, sighing through the green palms.
The people talked in joyous psalms;
Everyone wore a crown for
There was no one titleless
But princes, dauphins, infantas all
With pillows of paradise bird feathers
Fighting pillow-fights all day long
And dancing, singing until
The first ice in the central lake.
Then came the fir trees and the snows,
Then the birds the colour of shoes,
Then the mouths that cursed in prose
And the battles and the crows.
Until, at last, it did not rain;
The springy water that winds up
A land with liveliness and love
The Springs of Greenland ceased to run
And our lake lay beneath the mine
Miles deep of snow that covered the sun
From and away from that sweet place.

Come with me, my love, come down
To my lake in Greenland drowned
Beneath the centuries' years of snow
Beneath the tears that crystallized,
Come down and once more crown
Our heads with those days realized
In playing prince and princess
Before the snow
By a lake in Greenland
Long ago.

2. A City in Greenland

A bit too pastel, James, and written before
He'd explored the other half of himself
Represented by marriage and family
In which the landscape of the lost green land
Now covered with snow becomes a lost city
Of which Walt's Disneyland is a commercial
Monstrosity vulgar version. But this
Was a metropolis where we were the language
And the words were us.
Every once in a while I feel again
As if a word were trying to speak me,
And I feel myself changing into her
As the subterranean hyphen blurs into a river.

You ask why it is that language works,
And you say that it's because words are the directory,
The outline, the street plan
For a city we once lived in
And will again.
First I was a father's gesture
Accepted by a mother's Noun: Verb copula Noun.
If we talk the right way, we slowly story the city back
And release it from the two-mile prison of snow
That fell on top of it when the cosmic ruffians
Inside our planet rolled over in their sleep
And broke up Godwanaland into four drifting disjuncts.

You delight in the flutter shadows of leaves on pavement?
Those leafshadows are children playing there.
All sounds are the splashing of the Great Spring
Dancing up in their Market Square
Which they bit from, not drank.
Our sight is the tree, the tree that grew there
In whose branches we sing, the nerve ghost tree of blood
And nervous mycellium.
Our taste and smell were street cars and boats.
There was a tavern called the Noun.
And a gymnasium called the Verb.
Banks saved up prepositionings,
Bake shops sold stories you could eat,
And rich skunk histories,
Musk etchings,
Cinnamon in a stout cage
Our touch was the red lighthouse beacon
In a grasshopper's leg
With which we jump over death.

27

A man, I was the tongue of a woman.
Where is that city now?
Under two miles of historical snow.

What about me, said Venice, jealous.
Me the city of Money & Rialto,
And ducats & a wilderness of monkeys.
My cardinals carried pistols in fake
And hollowed out missals.
It was I thought of buying up the sailors' scrip
At a discount.
With the bushels of twists of paper,
I opened the first bank.
When they paid me instead of the drowned sailors
So impatient for drink & food & whores.
There was a special post box for letters
About traitors.
A penny bought a cow; clippers and forgers were hanged.
Because of me, actually, the young men did marry,
And the harbour is filled with ships.
Hear the jingle of me in most men's pockets,
Louder than the sound of their seed
Rattling in their secret alembics.
That too is the rusty voice of a God
We're still tuning.
Money is a sort of poem, said a poet in insurance.
I can get you back your city. Try me.

"Not without the right stories and the right words,"
A teacher says wearily. Once we were gestures and words,
We were their currency. Outside the Ojibway psychiatrist's
Window, a youth throws rocks at his window from the windy
Parking lot, slowly changing in John MacLeod's play
Into a lynx, the psychiatrist's forgotten totem
People used to hunt for new words with special masks.

Even, there was a mask you wore,
So you could creep up on good masks
And possess them.
In huge lexical arenas, we used to watch the myths
Fight each other. Jewish storytellers with their pit bull
Jehovah wiped out Odin and Wall Street.
Naked Eddas wrestled with a burly Jesus.
The American Wild West painter, George Caitlin,
In a censored page (folio reservatus) of his big book
On the Indians of Missouri, tells us of the Mandans
Who were ruled by a wily chief who used to disappear
From their midst at a certain time of their year

When the young braves were told their god would appear
And he did, dressed up fearsomely with a huge phallus
With specially horrifying glans. It was the old chief, of course,
Dressed up and disguised, walking in from the surrounding
Prairies. In his mask he scared them into civilized behaviour
For another year. That more or less is the way parents
Bring up families, screamers about "truth" to the contrary.

Instead of hunting, we had philosophy — Socrates hunts
"The deer of justice," if you remember *The Republic*.
Instead of fighting we had athletics, of course, and
Pretend massacres in rotation.
Life imitated art, as Oscar said.
We had scriptures instead of chromosomes

And continental drift and snow destroyed all this
In some sort of creative cycle?

Apparently, and yet I've seen it regained in simple ways:
You overhear a busperson say: "We do a lot of roller skating."
There is a grocery list crumpled on the floor.
Motes of dust gold in the sunladder slanting in the window
Which deal out another yellow window on the floor,
My father, long ago, asleep on an overstuffed sofa
Made by Kroehler,
A plate of wax fruit on the buffet.

At such moments, the planets are no longer pellets
Nor the sun a nuclear furnace, stones in space, ugh!
But as seen in time, our sun and her children are a long
Comet banner not unlike a great cuttlefish
Streaming through the dark, oceans as scarves,
The table cloth after the wedding of cloud shadows
Darkening, lighting up, darkening the road
Our bicycle glides down
This morning.

3. Greenland Dancers Danskers Dancers: For Two Voices

*The following poem is meant to be chanted aloud by two groups who work out among themselves
how to shade things in and out, but generally speaking the left-hand column provides a stereoscope
effect as in the double picture in stereopticons. I'm thinking right now of a long poem which can be
easily memorized from secret controls held in the hand — maybe the separate phases of a cat's cradle
string game. A great deal of dance can be added and sounds of all sorts if it's all kept moving like
mad, though. The Greenland in which the dances take place is as it was before the Ice Age; so really
green with palm trees and orange groves, no doubt.*

Greenland, there were dancers, dancers, dancers	Greenland Greenland Greenland
Greenland you were dancers, dancers, dancers	Greenland Greenland Greenland
There were no	men
There were no	women
There were no	children
There were no	fathers
There were no	mothers
There were no	you's
There were no	me's
Because the kind of I's saw those differences	There were nosssssssssssss's at all
Those eyes were the tickets you gave in at the door	Even both eyes, please thank you
If you wanted to dance on that Greenland floor	Prance on that Greenland floor
Greenland, Greenland, Greenland	Greenland Greenland Greenland
I'm tired of being who I am	Tired of being who you are
What was it you were anyhow?	Star star star star star star
Evening star I'll change you to	Do do do do do do do do do do
I'll change myself into to to to	Change Change Change Change
The shuffling rough gruff dust upon	A speck of dust upon upon upon
The trampling half blind twilight	Where has my star gone?
The trampling half blind twilight	The trampling blind twilight
Beggar's shoe	Beggar's shoe
You could dance like a beggar	Dance like a star
Dance like a speck of dust	Dance windrush
Dance like the twilight	Dance like the noon
Still as a stone in a field	All alone thinking, thinking
Whirling like a top	Never stop, never stop
Turn turn turn turn turn	Spin spin spin spin spin
Mmmmmmmmmmmmmmmmmmm	Nnnnnnnnnnnnnnnnnnnnnnnnnnnnnng
Oh!	Ohhhhhhhhhhhh! Ohhhhhhhhhhhh!
Greenland Greenland Greenland	Landgreen Landgreen Landgreen
I want to dance on that redhot floor	How much are the tickets?
They are no more, if you'd be wise	Than both your eyes
Here's my right eye	Here's my left eye
Why	Why
Now I see them dancing and I understand	There are stars nailed to his boots
Am Dancing	Dancing am
In	Greenland

Greenland
Greenland

———◆———

SERINETTE

"Serinette: petit orgue mecanique, a tuyaux et a cylindre, actionné a l'aide d'une manivelle, et dont on se sert pour instruire les serins. Par extens. Personne qui chante de routine et sans aucune expression."

(Nouveau Petit Larousse Illustré 1951)

"Un dictionnaire sans examples est un squellette."

I

There was a mocking bird in William Faulkner's orchard
Could do anything that his gramophone could & dared
Symphonies, string quartets. Oriental gongs, pianoforte,
Harps and even from nearby Memphis, Elvis Presley.
The mimicry
Drove the author crazy with its instant pickup in a minute
Of jazz, funeral march . . . . serviette, minuet.

II

Serinette, yes, the bird box
The small mechanical organ
Some farmer found in his barn near Sharon
And brought into the museum.

Serinette, yes: what you taught your canary
To sing Donizetti and Meyerbeer with;
More or less a musical saturationer
Played over and over again until the bird replies:

Janis Joplin, Elliot Carter, Ludwig Beethoven,
Petrouchka, Two Part Invention, Firebird.
My own little song which was my soul I've long forgotten.
I'll sing whatever you want, sir, if you'll stop
Turning the the handle handle of that mechanic organ
With pipes and a cylinder specially fitted
To mimic the latest: CBC Stereo trying to teach us
Even the Tintangel Suite, Arnold Bax, Rhapsody Cornish.

Meanwhile CHUM & CKSL grind their serinettes
Of Top Forty, Top Ten over and over again,
A special station in the States does Beatle songs
Over & over again & over & over again,
And eighteenth-century German soldiers
Marched to battle singing four-part harmony,
And Muzak in the Atlantic & Pacific stores
Sirens you to reach for Brillo pads and *floçons de riz.*

Serinettes of various sorts, we love you,
But we stop you now and listen to the silence.
What did we sing when we were a bird newly arrived
In this wilderness?
If we could go back and find the Irish fiddler & and Scottish,
The Kentucky & and Acadian, pebbles in our eardrum ponds,
Old hymn tunes John has found
Named after, of all places — Toronto! Cobourg! Darlington!

Those I sing this evening encourage and do this,
Though no doubt belittled in the *Star*,
Meeting craggy resistance in the *Globe*,
Hit with mallets, even hectored by the Charlesworth shades,
Told that "it is almost a work of genius, but not quite."
These I sing
This evening
Who unravel
Who unbaffle
The trail from the forest to the lawn,
From the bush to the salon,
The buried stream that flows from then
To today when without the bird organ
We tattle our own rattle,
Hum our own drum,
Ding our own gong
Sing our own song.

OH ALAN DAYTON

Oh Alan Dayton,
What has your hand done?
You have called up from fleeting life
To this exhibition, husband & wife,
Called them up to your bright vision
After shooting them twice in their garden
And letting them harden & flatten
In an ektachrome box's battering emulsive batter.
Then you copied that in these bright colours
Why, you have even called up from the grave
An ex-Dean of Women from Western.
Janitor & janitress of a Huron St. house,
We thank you for recording us.
When I was young, Stratford people said:
Reaney, will you ever be serious?
Now, may they come & howl
How I have learnt to seriously scowl!

THE CITY OF SECRET PROPORTIONS

The streets are empty in the middle of the night.
Leaves talk to themselves, streetlights
Shine on and on.
Graffiti, ads and trim-detail, Eraser Night dims out
So that I see only the *shapes* of the buildings.
I see the Parthenon's Golden Section
In this railway worker's cottage.
Neither he nor his wife nor his babe nor his carpenter
Know why they are so happy with a house that floats
Out *up* from its cellar, nor do the Cains and the Cahalans,
The O'Briens and the Pestalozzis know why the walls
Of Immaculate Conception Separate School,
With their faint low relief arches, make you feel triumphal.
& Roma!

Parallelogram factories where Miss Perspective twists out
A hurdy-gurdy tune; stairs, verandahs, gables
With rounder than round windows
Sing out their patterns, their secretly pleasing
Measurements

So that my town is made of temples where live priests and priestesses
Whose every act, from having a bowel movement to picking up
A crumb
From off the floor
To closing a door,
Is religious.
If the knotweed, the plantain, the poverty grass
In this vacant lot could be threshed *now*,
The town would never starve.

Near the Iona Fish and Chip Shop
A piece of newspaper crumpled into baby shape,
Rasps softly down the sidewalk pushed by the winds
The new day sends before him. The lights weaken?
Air tastes of a bell about to ring.
I dare myself to hear a toe or a wheel.
Yes, the driver of a load of pigs from Mitchell
Puts her in neutral and glides down the hill
That leads into my city of secret proportions,
Each pork crystal gruffing and yumming,
Gliding towards a hot dog tomorrow at Schneider's Meat Plant
23 miles away in Kitchener.
A boy on dope with a baseball bat will herd them up the ramp.

33

MARCH:
MELOS

One way of making your poems performantic is to have brilliant composers set them to music. We begin with *Souwesto Anthem*, something my son and self made up in the car while remembering the hurt we had suffered when a European neighbour had laughed at our region for being so flat. David Boothroyd set our poem with the Freedonia anthem from *Duck Soup* in mind. *Houses in Heaven* (John Beckwith) and *Advent Hymn* balance Methodist country chapels with that most tragic of churches — St. Patrick's in Biddulph. Jay Bowen set *Advent* when we were rehearsing *Handcuffs*, but all it needs is a liturgical shove. *Names & Nicknames* (Kenneth Winters) is originally set in Brocksden schoolyard, not far from Stratford; *Serenade* (Beckwith) would give audiences a chance to see what wedding serenades could be like in our area; the custom of Shivaree must be the only dramatic ritual put on, beside that of Hallowe'en, which doesn't demand help from the Canada Cow. Alfie Kunz set the two Christmas songs from *Let's Make a Carol*; James Brown of the same town, Kitchener, set the big solo that opens *I, The Parade*, a musical comedy about Professor Thiele, the musician who made Waterloo the musical capital of Canada. With the two songs from the detective opera, *Crazy to Kill*, we fall into the very sinister world of Souwesto seen from the viewpoint of a madwoman, adapted from a classic crime novel written by Stratford's Anne Cardwell in 1941. The last song, set by Mark Verwymeren, shows the same city just before the spectacular 1933 general strike that brought the army with machine-gun carriers to put down the riotous Bolshie throngs.

So this month ends with a vision of Souwesto that admits all is not pastoral delight; however, I decided to bring in the *Sleeping Giant* chorus here (Kunz), in which the Trickster Sleeping God at Fort William may awake with a solution.

35

—————◆—————

SOUWESTO

The scene: an Arts Faculty lecturer in the U.C. Drama Workshop.

DEAN SCHULTZ
Ladies and gentlemen, it gives me great pleasure
this evening to chair the last Faculty of Arts
lecture for the current academic year. Our speaker
this evening is that well-known geographer — Edwige
Doctor Edwige Sharples from the University of Leeds.
Dr. Sharples is renowned for her studies of the
physiography of Tibet and the tectonic origins of Switzerland.
Tonight she will give us the result of some two years of
intensive study on location: The Physiography of Southwestern
Ontario. Dr. Edwige Sharples.

SHARPLES
Southern Ontario is at the best of times and
the best of places an area of modest relief

The bedrocks of southwestern Ontario are among the
oldest beds to harbour the petrified remains of plants
and animals

This lack of faults carries with it the comforting
implication of a freedom from earthquakes

The slides begin — improvise around the following pattern:

flat — yes, monotonous — without relief
the snow helps a bit particularly if it's drifted
to any height what is the expression? flat as a
pancake *laughter*. No, I hardly consider that worthy
the name of either a depression or a hill — that —?
of course, it's a mountain, but it's some prankster, some
damn prankster has dished in a slide of Mount Fujijama
in Japan. Upside down you say? Again, the
prankster strikes. My young assistant who took these photographs.

Even my pet parrot who accompanied us on our tour — these
slides represent the topography of Essex County — what
you people over here call Essex County — my parrot would
say — flat, again — no relief, flat, yes, flat, flat.

*By this time the audience are advancing towards the
lecturer whom they assault with the following
anthem:*

It is not flat! Don't you dare call it that!
Souwesto! Souwesto! is where God hath sat
With holy bottom fat
Leaving ups and downs, villages and towns,
Eskers, kames and moraines, municipal drains
Dingles, dells, ravines,
Berms and muddy streams, Niagara Escarpment!
This place was never meant to be insulted
By that word* you've just used sir.
A complete misnomer!
Souwesto is not flat!

*"flat"

One of our neighbours rented their house for a year to an Englishman who, after introduction, opined that the countryside around London, Ontario was rather flat. Further developments with this chap involved the fact that my wife rings a rather large cowbell from the back porch if I am at the back of the lot gardening — 250 feet back, by the way. The ringing of this bell sometimes seemed to bring him out to his back porch in a fury. I think it did so because it sounded like the bell in a certain prison camp in Malaysia during the last war.

«Emblem for the township of my birth»

SONGS FROM OPERAS & PLAYS

HOUSES IN HEAVEN

Our Lord has prepared for us
Houses in Heaven.
How many rooms have they?
They number seven.
And what will we do
In this Heavenly House?
Watch flowers come out
All the day through.

In his cellar you'll find
Cool milk and sweet wine
And those so inclined
May spend all the day there.
And what will we do
In this Heavenly House?
Whatever you want to
All the day through.

In the woodshed you'll notice
Trees chopped up ready
And fine dry split kindling
For fires all so steady.
And what will we do
In this Heavenly House?
Watch the fire burn
All the day through.

In the pantry you'll find loaves
That ravens have brought,
Loaves everlasting
All fresh and hot.
Our Lord has prepared for us
Houses in Heaven
With tables of wheat bread
Spiritually leavened.

In his parlour the carpets
Refresh tired feet
Like valleys of green grass
All dewy and sweet.
And what will we do
In this Heavenly House?
Always be visiting
All the day through.

And up in the bedroom
Four angels are bedposts
Who each with a gold broom
Sweep care from your eyes.
Oh what will we do
In this Heavenly House
Dreaming true dreamings
All the day through.

And in the seventh room should be
A pair of folded hands
Praising him who built for thee
A house that ever stands.
All children and cousins
All brothers and sisters
And fathers and mothers
And relatives lost,
Lost loved ones
Dear Faces
Will be with you there
If not here, there.

— Act II, *Night Blooming Cereus*, 1956

ADVENT HYMN

Advent shadows in December,
Violet branches on the snow,
Help the Christian to remember
This babe returns to judge us now.

— Act, I *Handcuffs*, 1975

SIX SONGS FROM *NAMES & NICKNAMES*

1

So spring on Farmer Dell's Farm.
The snow has melted, the snow has gone
Tra la la Tra la la Tra la la
The bare trees have put their green leaves on.
Tra la la Tra la la Tra la la
Knee deep knee deep knee deep knee deep
The frogs in the pond sing
Knee deep knee deep knee deep knee deep
The frogs in the pond sing.

2

A schoolyard a schoolyard a schoolyard
Where is the schoolyard
Where the ground is stamped hard
With the children's stamping feet
We're on the way to find it
Find it find it
On the way to school
Dew dust mud hail
Snow ice frost smoke
Road lane ditch track
Truant officer
Tree
Pebble
Water
Splash!

In the School Room

Desk bell map chart	What pupils do
Clock book slate globe	
Chalk paper ferrule ouch!	Read write parse solve
Blackboard children teacher printer	Think reckon think learn
Student satchel pencil crayon	Think listen think attend
Register ink-bottle dictionary	Study recite declaim —
	Recollect and reckon compose compute
	Recollect recollect recollect —
	Remembrance remember remembrance
	Calculate analyze

RECESS!

Recess recess! Games! games!
A schoolyard a schoolyard a schoolyard
Where the ground is hard
With the stamping children's feet

They stamp their feet, then break into a games sequence.

Crack the Whip!
Send them flying!
Prisoner's Base

Have kids on stilts, playing tug of war, etc.

Come pull away, pull away
Bull in the ring
My bar's made of gold
My bar's made of iron
My bar's made of steel
My bar's made of stone

Have actual skipping, but watch the knots in those ropes!

Skipping skipping. The girls are skipping
Rosy apple lemon pear
These are the colours she should wear
The boys are walking on stilts
I am a girl guide dressed in blue
Skipping skipping. The girls are skipping.

For the individual games and skipping rhymes, break the CHORUS up into groups.

I'm the King of the Castle!
Get down you dirty rascal
Blue bells cockleshells
Evie ivie over
My mother said that I was born in January,
February, March, April, May, June, July, August, September
A house to let apply within
A woman put out for drinking gin
I call in — *name the child.*
All in together girls
Very fine weather girls
One two three four five
Salt vinegar mustard pepper

———————◆———————

Cedar cider red hot pepper
Hide and go seek Hide and go seek
Eenie meenie, tipsy toe;
Olla, bolla, domino:
Okka, pocha, dominocha,
Eenie meenie minie moe:
O-U-T spells out and
OUT you must go

A child who is "It" counts up to ten and then yells —

Anybody hiding round my gool
Whether he be hidden or not
He shall be caught
One two three on Walter!

A schoolyard a schoolyard a schoolyard
Where is the schoolyard
Where the ground is stamped hard
With the children's stamping feet
We're on the way to find it

Stamping.

Find it find it
On the way to school
Dew dust mud hail
Snow ice frost smoke
Road lane ditch track
Truant officer
Tree
Pebble
Water
Splash!

3

Sunset in Farmwife Dell's kitchen.
Cups and Saucers. Spoons and forks.
Knives and plates. Tea in kettles.
Fire in the stove. Bread in the oven.
Plants in the windows. Wood in the woodbox.
Towel on the roller. Water in the pail.
Dipper in the water. Kitchen kitchen
Supper supper. Sunset sunset.
Sunset in Mrs. Dell's kitchen
Sunset in Mrs. Dell's kitchen.

41

━━━━━━◆━━━━━━

4

PUMPING SONG

Down underground it's cold as winter
Down at the bottom of the well
Pump pump pump pump
Pump pump pump pump
Up above it's fire hot summer
The sun like a golden butter nut
Pump pump pump pump
Pump pump pump pump
Pump up winter into summer
From the secret underground stream
That flows beneath us like a dream
Pump! Splash! Gurgle gurgle.
Pump pump pump pump
Gurgle gurgle gurgle gurgle

5

Stars on a frosty night
In the depth of winter
Stars on a frosty night
In the depth of winter

If each child has two flashlights, quite a few constellations can drift over the stage:
the Big Dipper, Cassiopeia's Chair and, last of all, Orion.

Shine on the sleeping fields
Sleep beneath the snow
On the trees turned upsidedown
Their sap sunk below
Orion, Orion, Orion, Orion,
The cruel sworded giant
Made of stars he marches on
Over the snowy world.

Stars on a frosty night
In the depth of winter
Stars on a frosty night
In the depth of winter

6

Spring on Farmer Dell's farm
The snow has melted, the snow has gone
Tra la la Tra la la Tra la la
The bare trees have put their green leaves on.
Tra la la Tra la la Tra la la
Knee deep knee deep knee deep knee deep
The frogs in the pond sing
Knee deep knee deep knee deep knee deep
The frogs in the pond sing.

— *Names & Nicknames*, 1963

«You Mummer!»

———◆———

TWO SERENADES

SHIVAREE MUSIC I

All: Mister and Mistress Quartz we serenade you dear.
We won't let you go to bed until you give us some beer!
      Shivaree!
Mister and Mistress Quartz, we hope your honeymoon
Will be all the sweeter for the quiet rollicking tune
      of Shivaree!
If you don't give us some beer we'll stay
12 o'clock. 1 o'clock. two three four — break of day!
      Shivaree!

*(The noisemakers make their noise. There is a short silence. Then
the balcony window flies open and Mr. Quartz emerges with a shotgun.)*

Quartz: *(from the open window)*
I'll give you lousy bums to the count of ten
To get off my property — or I'll shoot.
One two

Elmer: This isn't your property, Quartz.

Sam: It's the king's highway.
(They're actually standing on the road.)

Russell: And you give us beer.

Bo:
Jo: Beer!

Quartz: three four five six

Elmer:
Ned: Beer!
Russell:
Sam:

Bo: Don't
Listen to him, boys.

Jo: Give him another blast!

Quartz: Seven eight nine ten!

*(They have just played a few notes — rather dimly and timidly —
when a blast from Quartz's shotgun sends them all flying.)*

---◆---

SHIVAREE MUSIC III

	Ring that bell, Elmer! It should be my wedding bell!
Serenaders:	Ding dong diggi dong ding dong dong
Jonathan:	Blow that whistle Sam and blow the horn, That's for a baby that's going to be.
Serenaders:	Whistle, whistle like the wind. Blow for the bride and her lost bridegroom. Whistle whistle blow blow Ding dong diggi dong ding dong dong
Jonathan:	Shake that rattle *(to Jo)* for the seeds in our garden, Our garden that is going to be.
Serenaders:	Shake the rattle for a seed that will grow. Rattle rattle Whistle whistle blow blow Ding dong diggi dong ding dong dong
Jonathan:	Crash those cymbals *(to Russell)* to scare away the fiend! Opening the gate of our garden to be.
Serenaders:	Stay away devils and spirits of the dead! Crash crash crash Rattle rattle Whistle whistle blow blow Ding dong diggi dong ding dong dong
Jonathan:	Beat that drum for my heart that's beating Fearfully joyously fearfully.
Serenaders:	Beat that drum — Ratatatat Wham! Crash crash crash Rattle rattle Whistle whistle blow blow Ding dong diggi dong ding dong dong FIRE! Fire, Mr. Quartz!

— Act II, *Shivaree*, 1961

TWO SONGS FROM *LET'S MAKE AN OPERA*

1

CHRISTMAS MARKET IN THE SQUARE

And yet it is such a happy time,
Christmas market in the square.
Farmer's sleighs come sliding in.
ringing their bells in the frosty air.

The farmer's wife, who sells fat geese,
is stamping her feet with the cold:
From the gray sky falls the snow,
like feathers of geese she has sold.

Look at the boy carrying the turkey;
it's almost as big as himself.
A team of white horses come in,
white as the snow itself.

Oh yes, it is such a happy time,
Christmas market in the square.
Farmer's sleighs come sliding in;
their bells ring in the frosty air.

2

KING'S CROWNS AND SHEPHERD'S CROOKS
S.A.T.B.
A capella, if possible.
(*Only soprano solo on words — all other voices hum.*)

King's crowns and shepherd's crooks,
Wisdom and simplicity;
Come to Bethlehem and see
How a baby God looks.
Through the winter wild
We sing the Christ child.

Come to Bethlehem and see,
As a simple shepherd boy,
Bring to Him His first toy,
A heart that is carefree.
Through the winter wild
We sing the Christ child.

Come to Bethlehem and see,
As a wise old king,
Like a dead branch blossoming,
Found at last this baby.
Through the winter wild
We sing the Christ child.

King's crowns and shepherd's crooks.
Wisdom and simplicity;
Come to Bethlehem and see
How a baby God looks.
Through the winter wild
We sing the Christ child.

Repeat carol with all parts humming as Mr. Powell and children exit, taking candle with them.

BANDMASTER'S SONGS FROM *I, THE PARADE*

1

"I, the Parade!"

Left right three four
Mother   Father
Because of them
My heart's a drum

For as I've said

I'm a parade
I am a parade

Tykes that fought me
Patrick Kelly

Aloysius Sweeney

Lower East Side
Where we reside
Right turn left turn
Fifteen sixteen

Down at the Battery

With my horn
Early in the morn

To see if they'd hire me

In a pick-up band
For a parade that would land

Up in Central Park

Took the trolley back
And they hired me again
Took the trolley back
From Central Park
A quarter each time
And again and again —
Heaven's got to be made
Of parade after parade!

Just under twenty
Play this *con amore*
Girl with a cornet
Taught her to play it
Performed vows marital
Eloped on a bicycle
On a ferry to the park

Coloured lights after dark
See him proudly walking

My idol the March King!

♪

2

Play louder and faster
He made me a bandmaster —
John Philip Sousa —
He too a parade was a!

Here come ten years
We played country fairs,
Summer resorts
Tired dead
Booked ahead
Train whistle
Hustle hustle

Here come the pupils
Boys' bands, girls' bands,
Music night and day
We willed them to play
Drove the first Hudson
Ever seen in Maine
Live by my wits
Love the kids
Love wife

Love life

3

Being sick's no joke
No rooms, dead broke.
Can't you drum
Faster, you lousy bum
I never slow go
I live allegro
Walk fast, talk fast —
Leave States at last.

Train Whistle

There's Mr. Hasenpflug
Come to meet the chug chug
That brought me to
Waterloo.
I hear here, I see
Marching not so quickly
Up here in Canada

I'm forty-one, ah
At this float
I gloat

4

(*Spoken*)   That's the truck my music company shipped 20 tons of
school songs with to British Columbia via Panama Canal
in 1934.

There's the boy who dropped the cymbal in the quiet
part when we played at the Ex. You little devil, don't
you ever do that again.

There's my band.
There's Ada who played the piano for the same trombone
piece 97 times at the Festival for me.

Who's that kid with the cart and shovel?

There weren't any horses in my parade.
The boys at Bamberg wouldn't keep their coats on.
They said it was too hot. I used to, you know, I used to
be able to hypnotize them into obeying.
I'm getting old. *A glass hearse appears.*
Stop the parade!
No, you don't collect me for the ash heap.

That's not my hearse.
Reverse! No — go ahead.
Because it all begins again.
There's my mother and father
Left right three four
Mother   Father
And because of them
My heart beats like a drum/My heart's a drum

And I'll never be dead
I, Charles Frederick Thiele,
I, the Parade!

48

SONG FROM A DETECTIVE OPERA, CRAZY TO KILL

THE DETECTIVE'S SONG

Hey!
What's been going on here?
Don't you hide on me!
Am I in love with someone
I'm never to see?
What's been going on here?
I'm really upset.
You know that I love you

Tho' we've never met.
Come out, come out, my darling
Wherever you're at,
or I'll tip this funny rest home
This way and that.

That way and this way
Ev'ry night and day
Nothing can ever subdue
My love that's strong for you.

Hiding in this kewpie doll?
Sunlight slides across the floor
All right, I don't care at all
I'll hunt for you no more.
And hide on you: *you* see
If *you* can find *me*.
Only I can give you peace of mind,
Only I your tangle can unwind.

What's been going on here?
I'm really upset.
You know that I love you,
(*spoken*) For God's sake
Don't play so hard to get.
Come to me, my darling, come to me.
Don't you dare hide on me.
Nothing can ever subdue
My love so strong for you.
Laughs (Richard Widmark)

«Dutchman's Breeches»

PRIME SUSPECT CONFESSES

While I sat sewing in the garden, the
Lennox boy dropped a little snake onto
the bench beside me . . .

'Twas then and there Miss Lawson
Decided that young scamp
Did need a lesson taught to him
At the gravel pit's high ramp.

I pushed him down, 'twas rather fun
His mistake to correct,
And then more situations noted
That needed some improvement!

Behaving very foolishly
With you, Dr. Lennox!
Nurse Zimmerman, ah! he so well
Remembers her red locks.

Miss Jones at the desk had the keys
Her pretty back was to me;
Choked her and got what I wanted —
To Zimmerman — entry!

Coming back from rectification
Of this young maid misled,
I put the keys back in the pocket
Of Miss Jones who's still not dead.

Tim's turn next for insulting me,
You delphinium skulker;
Turned off my flashlight, jagged stone —
I, of rudeness revenger.

Now everything should have been
Much better at Elmhurst
Save for police spy, Miss Currie
Making it so much worse!

On the floor of this hall she knelt,
Her shoe off, rubbing a corn;
Hit her with the shoe, her own shoe!
Choked her till life was gone.

I needed a stooge — Amy Johnston,
She maundered near the doorway;
Amy, I said, let us go out,
For dinner on the fairway.

Now there's one thing more to do
For Elmhurst's mental health,
And that's to tumble from his throne
Our head jailer himself.

So much impressed has been Lennox
Of late by his own incompetence
That some seconds ago he left
This room, he walked thence

Through the lobby and up the stairs
To his quiet study cell
At whose desk he found the means
To do one thing well.

♩

THE GIRLS AT SWIFTS

Six o'clock
Morning fog
Women walk
To their job.

There's the twins — I think that's Sue:

Florence, Sal,
Jessie, you.

Thirty girls — in the mist

Disappear
Into Swift's

WHERE THEY'LL GRADE
EGGS ALL DAY.

Thirty girls
Caught in a trap
Chickens pick
And butter wrap

I look at eggs — thro' a little light.

I dream of them
Through all the night.

There's a crack — a medium A:

The birds are dead
The foremen say:

GO DOWNSTAIRS
TO WHERE THEY ARE.

*From time to time we sense the foreman's presence & overhear him "speeding" the girls on.
Then we catch a glimpse of him: tough, brutal, lording it over 50 girls.*

Time crawls by;
It's winter now,
Walking home
Thro' the snow.

◆

The darkning sky — I look up through:

The woman up there
Picks chickens too.

Down thro' the air — feathers floating —

But if they did not
In the spring

Give her a chance — to do something else —

then her heart
Would turn to ice.

So now she wraps
This morning fog

WE WALK IN
TO OUR JOB.

— *King Whistle*, 1980
Brick, Winter, #8

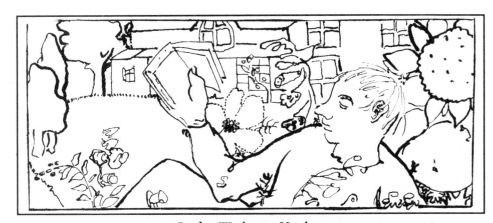

«*Reading* Wuthering Heights»

THE SLEEPING GIANT
(A short folklore sequence for a two-part children's chorus)

Near Fort William lies the Sleeping Giant,
Nanabozho is his name.
To his pillow we came,
He told us what has been, what is, what will be

I. *Choir speaks: "What has been."*
First the glacier covered all our country,
When it went back north,
Lonely were the forests and the prairies
Till we came with arrows, paths and guns and ploughs,
Villages, forts and towns, rail-roads, cities.

II. *Choir speaks: "What is."*
First there were the forests and the prai-ries,
Then we came with axes,
Cars and cows and taxes,
Sub-di-vi-sions, high-ways, trac-tors, ci-ties.
First there were the for-ests and the prai-ries,
Then we came with axes,
Cars and cows and tax-es,
Sub-di-vi-sions, high-ways, trac-tors, cities.
Now once the name-less rivers flowed are
Waterloo, Kit-chen-er and the Sault.
Medicine Hat, Saint Hy-a-cinthe,
Trail and Tru-ro.

III. *Choir speaks: "What will be."*
Last of all the Sleep-ing Gi-ant said
That in ten fields certain flowers he had.
As long as winds blow,
As long as waters flow,
We pray that Dog-wood, Prai-rie Cro-cus, Purple Violet, Pit-cher Plant,
Lady's Slipper, Trail-ing Ar-bu-tus,
As long as roads go, may these flowers grow,
Prai-rie Lily, Tril-li-um,
Wild Blue Flag and Wild Rose, Prai-rie Li-ly, Tril-li-um,
As long as the wind blows
Wild Blue Flag and Wild Rose,
May these flowers grow.

APRIL:
OPSIS

April is the month of competition festivals when, it used to be, British adjudicators came over and judged our singing, our Beethoven, our Bach, our rhythm bands, occasionally getting a chair hurled at them for passing over a favoured child, and occasionally running away with a young boy or girl to Australia. Well, have I confused Stratford with Vancouver in the thirties? There sometimes was a class for choral speaking, and what I am presenting you with here are poems that are meant to be orchestrated for spoken voice and any opsis and melos that come to mind.

In Riddle Competition, the solution might very easily be a solo voice over against fellow riddlers calling out their guesses on an improvised basis. These guesses are readings of the poems that might easily be a revealing of depths the author never thought of. To help a bit, I now add a list of answers, though not in the order their riddles are printed: Sun, the Wind, a Churchbell, phallus, gravestones (that are field stones), the Milky Way, Dawn, Water and Earth, churches, Twilight. In one case, the answer is the same for two riddles.

Pigeon's Neck refers to the brilliant mixture of metallic colours the male pigeon sports. One look, and I am transported past the Beulah mating world he is in, and beyond, to some other state. This, a very sensuous poem, is meant to make you swear "Jesus Christ" under your breath several times; some dancing and Song of Songs activity might not come amiss, with coloured slides, coloured lights. *Footnotes* has its own explanation. Try tape recording of footsteps, actors putting on different kinds of shoes and walking in them as loudly as possible. I can envisage a Foot percussion piece that begins with 100 bare feet and then, as in relays, participants put on footwear, go through a whole history of the foot, the sock, the shoe, the stilt, the clog, the slipper, the toed stocking, etc.

FOOTNOTES AND PODIATRY

This is a series of variations on the theme of the foot and its products — paths, roads, streets, steps in the snow &c. Part of it could be presented as a puppet show in which feet are mimed by hands that wear various shoes or pretend to be feet, or wear everything from rubber boots to spats to stilts and clogs. Or lower a curtain until there's *a very low stage at floor level*, where we see a line of feet. Select from the following:

1. How easily we read the town
    Complain those parts of us that up & down.
    How horribly difficult this muddy lane,
    To make sense of its slovenly gutturals.
    But, ah! there is a basin of hot soapy water
    Waiting for the ten-toed tired researcher
    At the end-of-it-all farmhouse they say,
    And a woodshed to leave these muddy spectacles
    To dry out their leather lenses in.

2. In the subway, hear the thunder
    Of the morning's million feet.
    Humanity's centipede
                Stampede
    To work above ground
        From sleep under.

3. In the nervous palaces of my labyrinthine mind
            Are neural nebulae,
    Bigger than the one we think's outside of us.

    I wonder is there a difference
    Between where the fingers live
    And the toes live?
    One a house, one a stable?
    Penelope's fingers wove, her toes treadled the loom.
    Krishna dances while he plays the flute,
    Makes love as well, to bring in another foot!
            I see them at night
            Asleep in their gloves
                and their spats beds,
    One dancer wakes up, conscious for his shoe.

4. FEET   Streets   Streets are
   Write   Make   Lined notepaper
   Street   Feet write   for footcaper
        Left, Right!   foolscapper.

5.   Snow is unlined vellum
For foot
In boot
    And toboggan, moccasin,
    Shewpack, raquette
      Sled

6. Despise the lowly foot
    At your peril.
It too is your mind.
And starts in your brow
Somewhere and somehow . . .
Someone says
Just above the eyes?

7. Street
Speak
Feet
Speak
Street

8.   Flake by flake
    And cell by cell
The Snowmen fall
The Snowgirls fell
Down down down down
    On the town.

9.   Look at all your feetnotes
    Behind you in the cement's
New ermine
    Covering.
Notes which are written
    By foot
In boot
By our feet
    On Snow Street

10. Bandaged by shoes
Blind five toes & his brothers
Read the street
Aloud
To one another
In a footfall
Braille

11. At night before I fall asleep
passing feet translate the street
        For me to dream about.

12. About this cement
Some footstep comment-
ary.

13. Passing feet Talk street.

14.   Street, you are
A cement bell
    Rung with fall
    Feet's footfall.

15. Dreams the serf street
    That
It
Walks upon our feet?

16. Students' swift shortcuts
Disgust the campus's
Dignified professor's
    Slower longcuts.

---◆---

17. Is it true to say that
    no feet, no street?
    When Roman pedes slept
    Under the vias, grass crept
        Yes, after a C years of no feet,
        Grass grows where chariot
            Once; though not
            Till even humbler knot
            -weed.

18. This short cut across
    Your lawn of legal grass
        Has
    Gagged and soft
    My footmouth.

19.   You, wheel?
    You, wheel!
    my enemy
        Rubber chisel
    Of freewail
    Of freeroar.

20. Street is dumb
    & speaks only leaf &
                styrofoam scrape.
            Now after twilight
            & no traffic,
                Night feet whisper
                    Of thief & madam.
                After midnight
                Some hopping paper
                Rustle, dead leaves
                When all feet & street
                Sleep.

21. Cows with their independent toes
    Of horn & cud philosophy
        Write primitive sentences
    Make their very own paths!
    By no means as straight as Roma's
    or the Lord's in Isaiah,
    Or the surveyors of Canada Upper
    Who followed the stars' whatever.

22.   Oh Pathmaker cow
        Carolingian cowbells
          You follow the lie of the land
  Like Gipsy roads though heavier,
  Your sentences all cobossed
      Together.
  And when the lead cow's dead,
        Why the next cow's path
        Is slightly different
  Across summer's pasture, but
  Still modelled on the Milky Way
      Which too,
        Shakily shook, &
          No doubt follows the lie
        Of the sky's
      Great gravity wells.
      Yes, they say the galactic highway,
    They say,
  Was pathed
    By a moo
  With a brimming udder
Oh, cow world so safe!
A milky cowpath
The highest thing in your sky!

23. These footsteps on my cellar stairs
    Make my head to raise its hairs.

24. Bare feet speak a flop drip sea-dialect
      Not the tough pen nib of cowhide copperplate.

58

25. Some feet read my staircase poorly,
    Some tick each syllable smartly.
    After the cleaning lady's waxed,
    Some swift readers read this course
        In crash bump cram!

26. Feet are handles in exile,
    Condemned to work in axle
    In mere travel
    When they would so much rather
    Have preferred to play the piano.

27. So late these steps on street outside
    Make me decide
    To get up and door bolt slide
    And think upon all night walkers,
        Their various breeds
        And their various deeds.

28. Someone has published these cement stanzas
    With hollow recesses
    So that my footsteps modulate
        Into
        Echo.

29. Marie Herbert used to take a shortcut
            Across Art McKone's wheat.
            He told her not to.
        She kept on, till school was let out.

30. Ah, the differing sounds high heels make
    I thought when sloppily my street
    Found a horsey voice of frail miss
    In recently bought Clydesdale-sounding
    High-heeled Bata clompers.

    Paths & roads
    Are the stories & odes
    Of our legs, ankles, soles & toes.

    My mother when uptown to
    Market also bought
    A special kind of
    Powder to stop
    The incessant creaking of a new
    Shoe,

    Everyone's feet
    Speak an ideodialect.

FINIS

Horace's ode where the slaves
Dance with their feet —
Feet tap
on the ground they hate
Because, though it be a holiday,
The soil makes them work so hard
And — oh, so few free days, so short!

I weep over a pair of shoes
My father wore,
When he worked as an orderly,
And am amazed at our babies' first shoes,
What coffinettes we teach their toetappers.

In going to school each day
Across a certain field
I, like the cows, eventually
Made my very own path.
Where it hits the eaves of our bush,
The fag end of it still visible.
My father said, never do that on
        Other people's property, Jimmie.

RIDDLE COMPETITION

1. With Distant Latch
    Of Coral slate
    The widow shuts her purse of stars.

2. Gone for a drink of water
    Gone for a drink of water
    Is the golden cluck
    Whose eggs lie above
    In their night-nest
    Of straw stars.
    Only one's hatched,
    Enormous graphite geo,
    Mother Earth,
    The one in the sun's sky now
    On which we are mites: parasites:
    Slavery & murder
    Storm & eyes.

60

3. A street in the sky,
   Dim,
   Bovine,
   Pathway of souls,
   Ancestor of this Irishman's lane
   Beneath my feet
   with soft shoulders
   and shirt of gravel complainers.
   Both of you guide me
   And bear me to town
   This night & back.

4. Eleventh finger,
   Eleventh toe?
   Shrivelled servant,
   Drainage outlet.
   Also stiff Emperor,
   Proud,
   Necessary visitor to
   Agdistes' garden
   Where with hermaphroditic
   Hoe —
   See the babies Dr. Macrae, row on row.
   My gun is better than your Gatling!

5. Without your presence,
   Puddle in the lane,
   No life, no suck, no muck:
   Great Hydro
   Humming on pole-wire,
   Gurgling in culverts,
   A married couple H_2O!
   Slippery & supple.

6. Here brought us glaciers.
   Those beneath?
   Their relatives' tears.

7. Who are you?
   Never have
   I that
   Out figured.
   Like the Pope in Wales,
   I bend down & kiss your field,
   Unlike him, jam myself
   Into a crayfish chimney,
   Horseweed, sorrel,
   Tickling my privates.

   All I know
   Is that you make
   Me Weigh 165 lbs.,
   And do not let me
   Jump too high.
   The higher I go,
   The swifter my deadly
   Slip & whump!
   When I expire,
   You'll swallow
   All of me,
   Not just this pronoun.

   All my nourishment
   Comes from your
   Marriage to the Sun
   Whom you dance into night & day,
   Seasons and time,
   Alma Mater,
   Accept my love.
   I stand up
   With the chimney still on me —
   A fleeting sour monster hag's uterus,
   Whom I have loved ever since
   Modelling her colloidal clay
   In the deserted brickyard
   When a boy . . . into portrait busts
   Of King George & Queen Mary.
   Crayfish, you matchmaker,
   Who made this clay condom,
   My favourite creek beast,
   Tomorrow, I promise you
   Fifteen grasshoppers
   As payment for your
   Strange services.

«My 21st Birthday Party»

8. In town, no one is awake
    Save one policeman
    On night duty
    And the guttering gaslight
    Not even allowed
    On nights with a moon.
    I search out the 11 sacred prostitutes
    To test their openness:
    Centennial Methodist, locked tight.
    Gospel Hall, shut up too.
    Congregational — no answer, legs forever crossed,
    And St. James — nothing doing,
    All asleep save the Coloured Christian
    Who's open to the sky,
    And will never shut again . . . deserted.
    Worshippers fled to Detroit.
    Only one lady takes me in,
    And she sits on the highest hill in town.
    By her flickering red candle light,
    I confess my crayfish experience
    To an invisible Jesuit priest:
    "Father, I've sinned with the earth."
    "Who told you to do this?"
    "The same voice which bade Ezekiel; 'To eat dung'."
    At the back, I ferret out their bottle
    And their bread box.
    I devour His body & His blood.
    Something I've always wanted to do.
    Am I a Man or am I not?

9. While pebble
    In an upside down
    Puddle of breath,
    Your ding
    Erases
    This demonic mythology
    And arabic astronomy.
    Your little dong goes ding!
    And shadows crack,
    Dark witch Luna
    Shows a fingernail of light
    Askew &
    Low in the southwest,
    A place
    Only drunkards & late nightwalkers
    See her in.

    Mercifully, Sleep
    Delivers a knock-out
    Blow.

10. You shadows cause
    But have none of your own?
    Enabling all who can to see,
    Yourself are blind?

11. You have a keyhole for mouth,
    My father's chimney for your pipe.

12. In fading overalls,
    In moonset bib,
    A Countless boy
    Plucks out some
    Cherries from
    A pocket of blue whistles.

PIGEON'S NECKS

Reader! No doubt you love
So naturally the shimmering mosaics
Of pigeons' necks.

Do you not cringe with wince
At the sharp flounce
And green fleck bounce
From grackles' wings?

Made they are
Of metallic ajar
Greens, Kelly and Maher,
Filched in the Sun's great square
From the Living Trees there.

Perhaps you love violence
When imitated, not acted out.
And so ache upon

The crackle glacé
Of crushed mica scales.

Loving gurgly babes
Makes you of glass candy containers
Slaves to colour differences of
Red candy through frosted green glass,
Green candy through frosted red glass,
A crystal bride and bride groom
Filled with glazed violets?

Oh pastels, just on the verge of marriage,
Their collapse into vulgar primaries
Just a microtone away, and yet . . .

Crinkled Xmas decorations,
Magnets of pink magenta.
Looked at in attic in July.
In Guatemala 299 different
Shades of orange burnt.
My senses completely derange
At the thought of slightly burnt orange
& less & completely & just one microphoton less than . . .
The radar of gentle slow, slow love.

Damn you, philosopher,
For saying I am frivoleer.
Did not the mystic cobbler,
Jacob Behmen,
Make a complete religion
Out of a coloured flash from a sunbeam
Smacking a pewter kettle upon
Its accidentally dinted brim?

In all this greasy dark carbon
Candle *non*-perception,
Lurks a sudden sparkle
That hark! it will
Delight
Ignite!

July, after dinner, alive
Despite the heat of the summer of 1935,
Lounging on a couch, sunlit, dog-
Day weather, and in Eaton's Catalogue,
Between my parents napping,
The paint and dye colours from which to choose:
Art shades, Nile greens, Chinese reds, écrus —
Egg shell brown: in the radio distance, hilarious
Watanabe, the Scientific Houseboy, set upon the isthmus
Of Singapore, this serial. Candies advertised in glass containers
In the shapes of frosted green railwaymen's lanterns.
Oh! Fundamentalist Materialism — awake to the cannonade opposite of heck
In the palace of a bird's small feather
Glittering green pink metallic tinsel,
The acid shades of neon
In Baton
Rouge, Louisiana.
In Brazil, mauve tropicana,
Off pinks.
Stupid ginks
Who live in raw dirty colours

Smeared by young talentless asses
In ignorant painting classes,
Come to the rinks of real,
Of Ice Cream colours,
Of chalk colours on pavement
Glazed in rain raiment
Or in conversation candies,
Sherberts, icings, clothes for babies,
Bridesmaids. Cakes in bakery shops
With bride and groom on micro honky tonk tops:
After the cake is cut,
All the pastels he jut
S to the primary supersaturation shift.
I've done it myself and yet need a last rift
Between me and the black of total blackout
Which dawn light fills, and yet must succumb
To noon and blowsy Day-glo.

Yet every night in sleep regain
   Virgo's
   Garden
   Under
   SNOW
& start again with ivory, bone white, paper white . . .

. . .

To be initiated slowly by the left
   Shoulder of "The red
   Streak
That heralds the day."

. . .

Bronze bright speckles on cheap wall papers of the thirties
My mother bought. In certain lights
   I faint . . .
   I tears rain . . .

MAY:
FACTA
St. Angelos Temporalis

One valuable source of public poems you put together on your own, perhaps as a conscious-ness-raising project for your community, is a collage of excerpts from the local writers and artists; the history of your apartment building before it became one; a report from Overhear-ing Oswald (the auditory equivalent of a Peeping Tom) who combs the shopping malls with a tape recorder for absurdist dialogue. Alice Boissonneau, in researching Parkdale for her novel, *Eileen McCullough*, discovered a lady named Ravina — why? — because she started life as a foundling baby in a Toronto ravine! Apply the techniques available in my *Donnelly* trilogy or *Colours in the Dark* and you're away.

As examples of ready-mades or *objets trouvés* — material which you assemble without changing it very much except to excerpt, juxtapose, and edit — I have chosen two modest sources — that of a weather diary I once kept for four months in 1939, and a journal kept by a local farmer in 1846 from which I have selected a very compressed "year."

After re-reading the weather diary, my insight about its re-arrangement is that it will be important to get the feeling for the various weather cells revolving like nebulous, ragged, battered tops made of cloud, winds, and moisture as the wind shifts in the first few days of 1939 from south, to west, to east, to north, to south again; then I would cut loose for weathervanes and rings around the sun and the moon, as well as the appearance of my favourite celestial, the Sun Dog. Use slides of sunsets and clouds; imitate the local wind sounds.

You may use other people's weather diaries and journals — these abound in local archives. Or you can set aside a year just to keep either or both of your own.

"What shall I write about?" I am often asked. Keep a record of yourself and your community, a daily record. One day, take a look at what you have been collecting, be it weather or passersby on the street, or a review of all the clothes you have ever worn — the passage of the angel of time ensures that what once seemed so banal and commonplace will quickly become that magic thing; the past, remembered and organized by the humblest of formulas — the patient daily record.

67

WEATHER FOR 1939: EXCERPTS

JANUARY

1 Sunday — Wind — South/Weather — cold, snowing slightly/Sky — Cloudy

2 Monday — Wind west/weather — milder, snow towards evening/sky —
   cloudy, nearly cleared away in the morning.

3 Tuesday — Wind — east, a sleety and very cold wind/weather — very cold,
   snow deep hard to get around/sky — cloudy.

4 Wednesday — Wind — south east/weather — very cold wind, blowing snow
   around a lot/sky — cloudy.

5 Thursday — Wind — south/weather — mild, thawing raining heavily/sky —
   cloudy, sometimes clearing away. Thawing.

14 Sa — Wind — west, Weather — clear, sunny/sky — blue

15 Su — Wind — west/weather — cold, snowing slightly/sky — cloudy.

26 Th — Wind — south east/weather — cold more moderate/sky — clear, a kind
   of a haze. Ring round moon.

FEBRUARY

8W — Wind — west/weather — mild, very, thawing, flooding/sky — cloudy
   partly, sometimes clearing.

MARCH

18 Sa — Wind — northwest. Sun Dog/weather — snowing in morning, clear in
   afternoon/sky — fair.

20M — Wind — north west/weather — cold, windy but in sheltered places it thawed under
   warm sun. Snowed awful at four o'clock cleared at evening/sky — cloudy.

28 Tu — Wind — north west/weather — cold wind, frosty except at noon/
   sky — blue in morn — cloudy at sunset.

APRIL

1 Sa — Wind — west/weather — rainy, muddy raw/sky — cloudy.

25 Tu — Wind — south east/weather — very warm and cloudy at evening/
   sky — fair and blue, red sunset.

29 Sa — Wind — north west/weather — cooler but lovely at times/sky — blue.

30 Su — Wind — northwest/weather — cooler, warm and sunny at noon./
   sky — sometimes cloudy, blue

«New Mouth Organ in the Orchard»

————◆————

WILFRID THOMPSON:
Self Portrait

His farm was at the Little Lakes where the Old Huron Road makes a Deviation Line to avoid a bog and hits another bog, by McCarthy's Lake instead of Jones' Lake. Over the former was built a floating bridge from which a circus elephant, seven teams of horses, and one Irishman dropped to bottomlessness (the story teller's word) — dead, ghost, etc. Thompson cleared the farm Robertson (see *Imprecations*, an earlier poem in this book) had such difficulty in protecting from the encroachments of Marty Halpin. Aside from the surveyor's notebook, this is the earliest record of our neighbourhood. Like a swallow, skimming into his own pond of old, dry ink, I return with the following:

JANUARY 1846

Some person has been in the West Barn today
      no whiskey in the village
            thrashing wheat
Emily & the boys to make calls in Brocksden &
On John Stewart & the Crerars.

February Nomination meeting at Stratford
      Erb — a young Prussian
      Duke & Diamond — yoked steers for first time

March Tapped 55 trees & placed sugar troughs
      Tom hauling rail timber
            saw first bluebird
Called up about 4:40 a.m. by Mail Driver Wilson who borrowed Charley to help him to Stratford, one of his horses being
Knocked up. Roads impassable. Tom has just expired, Fits.
Washed & did the needful to his corpse.
      A black man from Hamilton & his son (& his Horse)
      for the night

April Saw first swallow
      A Hamilton teamster & Pedlar begged accommodation
      for self & Horses the other night

May — Thursday 28
      Hauling manure yesterday — Denny in Garden
      forenoon — afterward to Stratford for yeast —
      none to be had — sowed Cabbage in Hotbed —
      Thyme and Mary in West Currant Border.
      Wilfrid to Peter Crerar for five Bushel of Potatoes
            2 Teams with Emigrants Stopped
                  Deer south of clearance

69

June Leeches sent by Mr. Norton with a passenger on the Stage

July Apples stolen — eastward
     A Pedlar had accommodation for self & horse

August   trade in Holly hock seed for Tiger Lilies Mulberry
          on the lake for grunters

September   wolf killed lamb
        gathered snow apples
        Ploughing Match   Hyde First Prize 10$

October   1 1/2 hours — lunar rainbow/bright Rocket falling star

November took Lyra to the Bridge wont go over it
        Hauling the waggon off the Bridge — up to knees in
        mud hole

December took 3 drunken Indians home to wigwam on ox sleigh
        trapped a fox   3,000 sheaves — thrashing

Somewhere else in this journal, Thompson uses the phrase "en passant" — which must have been
the first time it was written in South Easthope, my township.

«Elm   Tree Love»

JUNE:
POETICS

In the month of final examinations, we present a toughie, a performance poem inspired by a scholarly book, Francis Yates' *The Theatre of Memory*. It's a story of the perils that afflict those who reject myth and metaphor (the gods) in their art, in their religion, in their family and in their society.

The times were propitious. Umberto Eco had just published *The Name of the Rose*; even the little book he then wrote about how he wrote *Name of the Rose* — line up the archetypes & formulae — was a bestseller! I had been asked to lead a workshop for teachers that would have as its subject the Globe Theatre, Shakespeare's chief venue with "All the world's a stage" its motto, and Heaven, Middle Earth, Hell its architectural plan. The Development Day workshops were being held in the auditorium of the Stratford Normal School just across from another theatre deeply influenced by the Globe's design — the Stratford Festival Theatre.

The way it is influenced, by the way, is the theme of the accompanying playlet — actually, a playlet-lecturette!

If you think of a typical theatre forced upon us by this most materialistic of all the centuries, regard a cinema in which you are separated from fellow members of the audience by darkness; the stage is a window upon which shadows dance, but you can't climb out of this window. There's a wall behind it and no living beings, no dressing-rooms, only a tired projectionist, some ushers, and perhaps some of the creeps that inhabit that Tennessee Williams short story, *Hard Candy*. Even this is fading away — at least you had to walk to it, and there were fellow human beings, even if you never saw them properly; switch to the nineties, when our typical theatre is a bed upon which two people lie — one trying to sleep, the other slugging it out with their third VCR movie of the night — what about *Texas Chainsaw Massacre*?

By way of contrast, the Elizabethan theatre got you out of the City and across the river and, if you didn't choose the Bear Gardens, into a closely packed daylit (matinees used to be in the morning, remember?) arena in which the whole building stressed a multi-levelled universe with love-goddesses such as Juliet and Cleopatra up there, groundlings and tragedians on a middle earth stage, and underneath, through a trap door, the cellarage where demons and ghosts lurk, tempt you to kill your uncle, during which process you kill seven others (some of them totally blameless) besides.

In this century, we may revive this kind of theatre, but we, in the mass, tend to think in terms of Caliban's wished-for bookless island where, without even a witch to provide some variety, he sits huddled in front of the Cyclops eye of VCR and Cable and Satellite's 150 channels.

Therefore, this play focuses a group for discussion of how we produce symbolic art and architecture once more. Readers may like to read Colin Still's *Shakespeare's Mystery Play*, which gives you new slants on *The Tempest* as a purveyor of poetics for popular audiences. *The Wasteland*, said to be Eliot's best play, is also said to have been influenced by Still's book; you might like to add parts of both to this script. Also Hugh Kenner thinks that Eliot started out by creating a medley based on *The Aeneid*, Book VI.

Art as mentor of spiritual depths and heights, of rebirth, of combating the boredom of our capitalist, phoney paradise — see if you do not herein find some new ways out to more genuine cities in emulation of the new Troy Aeneas left Carthage to found.

In short, here's a chance to get out of a building about to tumble down. A messenger has arrived with the news that two strangers wish to see you — outside.

«Campus Literate»

A TRIP TO THE GLOBE THEATRE

19 October 1984   Normal School Auditorium

VOICE I   A nobleman of Thessaly, named Scopas, gave a banquet at which the poet Simonides chanted a lyric poem in honour of his host. But the poem also spoke highly of those twin sons of Leda and Zeus — the Heavenly Twins, Castor and Pollux.

SCOPUS   Too much about Castor and Pollux. Half my money, Simonides, is being spent in singing about Castor and Pollux. How much did I promise?

POET   Sire, ten drachmas.

SCOPUS   Bah, I give you five! *sound of coins flung* And you must get the other five from your identical friends in the sky — Castor and Pollux!
banquet sounds

MESSENGER   Sire, I am told Simonides was reciting somewhere this evening — perhaps at your house, sire.

SCOPAS   The rascal vagabond poet — at the lower table — ask my butler.
banquet sounds

MESSENGER   Sir, are you the poet, Simonides?

SIMONIDES   Indeed I am that.

MESSENGER   Two young men, Simonides, are waiting outside to see you.

VOICE I   The poet rose from the banquet and went out, but could find no one.
sound of earthquake
During his absence the roof of the banqueting hall fell in, crushing Scopas and all the guests to death beneath the ruins; the corpses were so mangled that the relatives who came to take them away to burial were unable to identify them.
pause: music

SIMONIDES   Ah, yes, at the lower table — where I recited the poem — there was a circle of twelve; on my right, that fellow, *Anthropos, and, on his right, his friend, Biblos. Beside him, Krupto, then Daimon, Ergon, Gymnos, Hydro, Logos, Mania, Neuron, Orama, and the empty place where sat myself — the poet Simonides. Oh Castor and Pollux, how handsomely you have paid me for remembering to sing of the gods as well as men.
music

     * See Greek Roots/Etymology, or the Derivation of Words in *The Practical Speller*, W. J. Gage & Co., Toronto, 1881.

ST. AUGUSTINE	I look inside my mind, my soul, and find a great city. I come to the fields and spacious palaces of memory where are the treasures of innumerable images, brought into it from things of all sorts perceived by the senses. *music* Behold in the plains, and caves, and caverns of my memory, innumerable and overflowingly full of innumerable kinds of things . . . over all these do I run; I fly; I dive on this side and that, as far as I can, and there is no end.
CHORUS	**A GUIDE TO THE THEATRES OF LONDON, 1576–1642**
VOICE 1	On the city side of the River: *2* *3* *4* *5* The Red Bull, The Fortune, the Theatre, The Curtain, The *6* *7* *8* *chorus* Boar's Head, The Red Lion, The Cockpit — all outside the City Walls.
VOICE 9	— Actors are vagabonds. Actors may not be jurymen. Across the river: *10* *11* *12* *13* *14* The Swan, Bear Garden, The Hope, The Rose, The Globe.
FRANCES YATES*	— So might the vast inner memory cathedrals of the Middle Ages have been built.

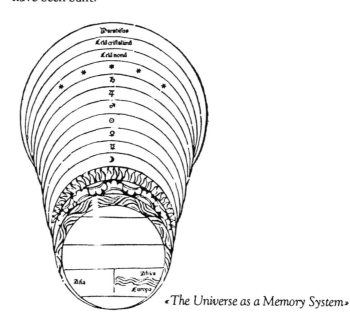

«The Universe as a Memory System»

* Frances A. Yates. *The Art of Memory*. Penguin: London, 1969.

CHORUS	THE SPHERE OF THE UNIVERSE AS MEMORY SYSTEM
15	Seraphim
16	Cherubim
17	Thrones
18	Dominations
19	Principalities
20	Powers
21	Virtues
22	Archangels
23	Angels
24	Crystalline
25	Primum Mobile
9	The Stars
8	Saturn
7	Jupiter
6	Mars
5	The Sun
4	Venus
3	Mercury
2	Moon
1	Fire

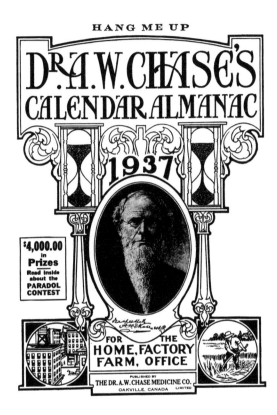

SIMONIDES	Air
MESSENGER	Water
SCOPAS	Earth — the Globe

YATES — in these theatres part of the stage had a covering which projected from the tiring-house wall and was supported by posts . . . the underside of this covering was painted to represent the heavens. There would have been representations of the zodiac with its twelve signs, of the spheres of the seven planets as well, and all called — the heavens. Hamlet points to this when he says "firmament fretted with fire".

1	2	3
HEAD	RAM	ARIES
4	5	6
THROAT	BULL	TAURUS
7	8	9
HANDS	TWINS	GEMINI
10	11	12
BREAST	CRAB	CANCER
13	14	15
HEART	LION	LEO
16	17	18
BOWELS	VIRGIN	VIRGO
19	20	21
KIDNEYS	SCALES	LIBRA
22	23	24
SECRETS	SCORPION	SCORPIO
25	2	3
THIGHS	ARCHER	SAGITTARIUS
4	5	6
KNEES	GOAT	CAPRICORN
7	8	9
ANKLES	WATER BEARER	AQUARIUS
SCOPAS	SIMONIDES	MESSENGER
FEET	FISHER	PISCES

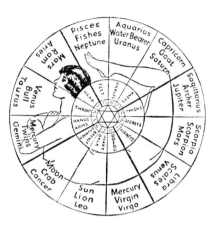

CHORUS   Hang me up / Dr. A. W. Chase's Calendar Almanac / 1937 / $4,000.00 in Prizes / Read Inside about the Paradol content

VOICE 2   For the Home, the Factory, the Farm, the Office

VOICE 3   Published by the Dr. A. W. Chase Medicine Co. / Oakville, Canada Ltd.

VOICE 4   "There is nothing like Dr. Chase's Nerve Food to restore pep and vigour to mind and body, to give you control of yourself and to bring the colour back to faded cheeks."

SIMONIDES   My first introduction to the idea of a giant in the sky who guarded us all was the picture in this almanac of a naked woman coiled in a circle, zodiacal signs stamped on her.

YATES   — The classical theatre, as described by Vitruvius, reflects the proportions of the world. The proportion of the seven gangways in the auditorium and of the five entrances on to the stage are determined by the points of four equilateral triangles *music to x* within a circle, the centre of which is the centre of the orchestra. These triangles, says Vitruvius, correspond to the trigona which astrologers inscribe within the circle of the zodiac. *x*

VOICE 1   Julio Camillo was one of the most famous men of the sixteenth century . . . His Theatre was talked of in all Italy and in France — what was it exactly? A Wooden Theatre, crowded with images — a certain Amphitheatre, a work of wonderful skill, into which whoever is admitted as a spectator will be able to discourse on any subject no less fluently than Cicero.

CAMILLO (*stutters*) It is, Signor, a built or constructed mind and soul . . . or a windowed mind and soul. All the things that the human mind can conceive are here in the images I have collected and arranged in my Memory Theatre.

CHORUS Mrs. Hester Thrale, in 1750, lived in London near the site of the Globe Theatre.

MRS. THRALE — A black heap of rubbish . . . they were really the curious remains of the old Globe Playhouse which, though hexagonal in form without, was round within.

SCOPAS (*sulkily*) The elemental world would be the square stage on which man plays his part. Four elements, eh?

SIMONIDES The round celestial world hangs above this — the vestige of the divine.

MESSENGER Above the heavens would be the supercelestial world of the ideas — the Seraphim.

CHORUS Enter Prospero above, invisible. *music*

ALONZO What harmony is this? My good friends, hark!

GONZALO Marvellous sweet music.

CHORUS Prospero discovers Ferdinand and Miranda playing at chess in his cell.

VOICE 15 Pawn to King 3.

VOICE 14 Pawn to Queen 4!

CALIBAN Remember / First to possess his books; for without them
He's but a sot, as I am, nor hath not
One spirit to command. They all do hate him
As rootedly as I. Burn but his books.

ARTHUR The wall is high, and yet I will leap down.
Good ground, be pitiful, and hurt me not.
Oh me, my uncle's spirit is in these stones. *falls: screams*
Heaven take my soul, and England keep my bones.

GHOST Swear by his sword.

HAMLET   Well said, old mole, canst work i' th' earth so fast?

YATES   A worthy pioneer.

MESSENGER   The above scenes from *The Tempest, King John, Hamlet* — show the complete range of the Globe Theatre, from the white magic of Prospero that attains Seraphimhood to the dark world that kills Prince Arthur as he tries to escape his wicked uncle, to the elemental under-earth where a vicious demon ghost lures Hamlet on to kill eight people instead of one, a great many of them innocent.

              However, there's no use being little Johnny Head-in-the-Air. Miranda and Ferdinand will marry; the downward drag of earth allows a base for a full life where the dancer's foot and the chessplayer's board is always confident of another step, another game. Camillo's Theatre of Memory, Burbage's Globe — are rooted in an earthy world of sensible sensuality that plays the complete harp from Seraphimhood to Earth as if it were our backbone — which indeed, spiritually, it is. Castor and Pollux, I pray you one last vision for my poet friend.

Thunder. Castor and Pollux represented by two blazing stars each:
CHORUS   Only the earth doth stand forever still:
              Her rocks remove not, nor her mountains melt;
              (Although some wits enrich'd with learning's skill
              Say heaven stands firm and that the earth doth fleet
              And swiftly turneth underneath their feet.)
              Yet, though the earth is ever steadfast seen,
              On her broad breast hath dancing ever been.

Bring in a TV set, a radio, both turned on to whatever is on in your community. Caliban slouches in with popcorn and beer. With a belch he says:
CALIBAN   You know — we did burn that old highbrow's books — what a pedant, just not living in the real world at all — always being literary. *pause* But the trouble is — we were all in his books, so that, as they burn up — why we catch fire.

He pulls a long streak of red silk fire from his pockets. Invisible black strings pull other such scarves until he is a mass of flame. After he becomes a heap of cinders, the heavenly twins thunder *move forward, sift up the dust with golden broom and golden dustpan — blow it away to a great glissando from Simonides' harp.* pause *The TV flickers, fades.*

We are left with the constellation of the heavenly twins — four blazing stars whose simplicity and order always add grandeur to the spring sky, where also float those other majestic sky figures — Virgo and Leo.

THE END

JULY:
CATALOGUE POEMS

There is something about lists of things that hypnotizes me — *The House that Jack Built*, or the sequence "and then the rope began to hang the butcher, the butcher began to beat the ox, the ox began to . . . and the old woman got over the fence."

I think this fascination is connected with our joy in the rainbow's week of colours, in the 92-element candle you see in a physics lab at school, but then see all around you like a segmented serpent we're all tied together by. Our backbones, with their xylophone vertebrae, are such sentences; lists of symbolic objects in some sort of mysterious, overwhelming progression I have called elsewhere the backbones of whales, and indeed they are, for they are capable of becoming a paradigm (Greek fingers on a hand as a mnemonic device) used as a secret structure.

Let's take the list of things and people in a popular carol, A *Partridge in a Pear Tree*: quite a good stage piece could emerge from developing the insight that the title itself is a peasant mishearing of a Latin carol about a "Virgo qui parturit infantem Christum"; in English, we have "parturition" for "giving birth." But, knowing no Latin, the folk mind makes the birthing word into a partridge! Try to find out about "French hens," why "four colley birds," and you've got a quarter of your Christmas Concert right there — if the authorities let you promulgate a religious myth any more, that is. Lately, I've noted a distressing tendency for Christmas concerts to be about Santa Claus and his relatives and entourage, only. No nativity plays.

Let's take another list: Light
Separation of Waters Above from Waters Below
Dry Land & Grass Rise up from Water
Sun, Moon, Stars
Fish, Great Whales, Birds
Animals & Man
He Rested.

The First Seven Days of Existence! It would be of interest to try to smoke out what modern science sees as its vision of the first days of existence. At any rate, while we're waiting for more story line here, let's work away at the Seven Days we have; in once doing so, I found that I soon had, with about thirty children, young people, parents, and babes, a stage piece called *Genesis*, the bare bones of which I here append.

GENESIS

Beginning with: Revolt of the Angels; War in Heaven

Sing: *Jacob's Ladder* — come in climbing the ladder

    (a)   Let's all go to Sunday School
          — hum, drum fingers on the floor for the rain
    (b)   The Minister reads the first verses of Genesis
    (c)   The People suddenly start chanting them
                  CHAOS! CHAOS!
    (d)   The People divide into the hands of God
           WE ARE THE HANDS OF GOD

On the:

    (e)   **First Day** — LET THERE BE LIGHT AND THERE WAS
    (f)   **Second Day** — HE DIVIDED THE WATERS
    (g)   **Third Day** — DRY LAND AND GRASS
    (h)   **Fourth Day** — SUN, MOON AND THE STARS
    (i)   **Fifth Day** — FISH, GREAT WHALES AND BIRDS
    (j)   **Sixth Day** — ANIMALS AND MEN
    (k)   **Seventh Day** — HE RESTED.
    (l)   **Singing:** *Big Rock Candy Mountain*
    (m) Adam and Eve get entangled with the Serpent
    (n)   They are banished from the Garden
    (o)   Cain and Abel
    (p)   Story of Lamech
    (q)   Adam, Seth, Methuselah and Enoch:

                  Adam lived for 930 years and he died,
                  Seth lived for 912 years and he died,
                  Methuselah lived for 969 years and he died,
                  Enoch lived for 365 years and he lived
                      and was taken to heaven on a chariot of fire.

    (r)   **Singing:** *The Old Ark's a-Movering*
    (s)   Everybody gets drowned except the good people and the animals
    (t)   Sacrifice
    (u)   Nimrod the Tyrant/Tower of Babel/Ur of the Chaldee/Abram

You might look up Milton's version of the Angelic rebellion and, of course, children will already know the version promulgated by the authors of *Superman I*; the Zeus and Prometheus story would be a good influence here, too. In the Sunday-School sequence, half the message is the flies buzzing on the windowpanes. Most kids prefer to be in the left hand of God, by the way, once you tell them about Good and Evil being twins. (Use Isabella Crawford's *Malcolm Katie* here.) "Waters above" needs some research; another sea was thought to lie above us, contained by a crystalline firmamental glass bell. Rain, particularly the Flood, was the result of openings in this firmamental bell.

Use a garden hose for the serpent. The Story of Lamech is that of the first manslaughterer; it's an influence on *Wuthering Heights*, has the idea of a seventy-fold curse, rather than just a sevenfold one, and should be better known. The essential situation is that a blind old man, Lamech, is tricked into shooting an arrow and, of course, kills a young man.

Use Addison's *Vision of Mirzah* to show the varying ages of the patriarchs. The Tower of Babel can be built of cardboard boxes found out in the alley; and the language explosion should be a cinch with all our recent arrivals from Hong Kong, Sri Lanka, Viet Nam, French Immersion, etc.

Using *Donnelly* techniques, and the combination of mime and percussive improvised commentary pioneered in my *Names & Nicknames*, see how all this water expands the dehydrated list I showed you at the beginning.

For good measure, I now add Professor Sheldon's list of the various kinds of male body shapes photographed in his *Atlas of Man*. I can't think of a story line just now, but I suspect that it's bound to appear the moment you get your catalogue of male bodies in your community lined up with the three major divisions in Sheldon's book; and they are:

walking-stick insects, thin as — *ectomorphs* — worshippers of the brain, apt to be wizards in our society, nervous individuals;

mesomorphs — the powerhouse types, worshippers of their own energies, aggressive, handsome soldiers, kings, knights — centred on the Big Cats in the list I've given you;

endomorphs — worshippers of the gut, big fat Buddha types, busdrivers, bouncers, happiest eating — hippopotami!

Of course, all of *us* are intermixtures of this trinity. In his other books concerned with the varieties of human temperament, Sheldon supports his analysis of the effects of this mixture on human lives by rivetting interviews and character portrayals.

I suggest that the endomorphic peasants have grown tired of giving most of their millet and corn to the aristocratic, handsome mesomorphic soldiers and knights, as well as to the priestly scribes and theologians. So they find, down by the muddy river bank, a class Sheldon admits having difficulty with — the outcast poets, artists, tinkers with their secret language, the untouchables. For a while, they win, until . . . ?

THE ATLAS OF MAN

Walking Sticks
Wasps
Flycatchers
Little Falcons
Big Falcons
Great Owls
Eagles
Stingless Mosquitoes
Dogs of the Near Southeast —
Brittle, Delicate, Lean & Fast
Dogs of the Near Northeast —
Lean and Fast, but Less Delicate
Little Cats
Great Cats
Supercats
Sandpipers
Railbirds
Rabbits
The Three-Four Dogs, or Mid-Range Dogs
Horses
Between the Cats and the Bears
Pleistocene Supercats . . .
Great Cats of Bearlike Proportions

Oyster Catchers
Marsupials
Sheep & Deer, or Whom the Dogs Hunt
The Four-Four Dogs
Bulls
Great Bears
A Superbear
Kiwis
Under-the-barn Kitties
Ant-Eaters
Oxen
Elephants
Rhinoceros
Auks & Penguins, Weak-Winged Swimmers
Seals
Porpoises
Walruses
A Hippopotamus
Manatees & Dugongs
The Mermaids
Toothless Whales
Whales with Teeth
The Sperm Whale
An Ancient Hippopotamus

Quite a bit of the catalogue philosophy invades my mental-landscape play *Colours in the Dark,* and the reader should look up the Set of Dishes scene for guidance. For twenty years, one idea I have longed to develop is the story of a kingdom in terms of its coinage — use museum slides; e.g., I think of those British kingdoms where the coinage got smaller and smaller as the Roman Empire receded into the past. Or why not try Ontario or one of those Anglo-Saxon kingdoms where you start with a dragon on your pennies (not unlike the wights Iceland still has) and end up with a king's face which is also the face of a saint.

Literally, ideas for catalogue sequences have been picked up in Goodwill stores — a hilarious set of records telling you how to fold sheets for Howard Johnson motel bedrooms in 1. 2. 3. &c. order; a discarded Harvey's training book that tells you how many times to pat the two sides of a hamburger, again in list format. When sorting out the contents of an old print shop in St. Marys some friends gave me, I came across ten cardboard shirt fronts with slightly different messages pencilled on each one, such as: back in 30 seconds, back in a minute, back in a few minutes, back in 5 minutes, back in a quarter of an hour, all the way up to closed for the afternoon, and CLOSED. Or, my wife in cleaning up Jack Chambers' studio, as a way of helping pay for a painting of his, discovered a pile of 500 lunch bags in a corner, discarded each day for two years.

Further ideas revolve around the lists to be made of commedia types of characters in Frye's *Anatomy of Criticism*, the notion that the basic plot of all dramas revolves around a dragon and a witch meeting up with a knight and a helpful dwarf who save a beautiful half of the knight's full self called, in William Blake, his emanation or . . . girl friend. To this add gracioso, agroikos, pantaloon, old, old women, really sweet ingénues (for the subplot); make the dragon into King Lear as hero, and the young mesomorphic knight into an Edmund (the eiron character is reversible) and you have the plot of tragedy, turn it again and you have romantic comedy.

Or try just a list of cars your father drove, from getting his first driving licence to now — and you have the story of Ontario in recent years — let alone the world of Grey County, Ontario in the nineteenth century, where male members of a certain family whose descendants I know implored their father to get some horses, no girl would be seen with them in an oxcart!

The catalogue is an exuberant, elastic structure, a segmented boa constrictor with which you can swallow your neighbourhood, your town, your province — tomorrow the universe!

«Edith Sitwell with Cello»

AUGUST: PRIVATE PUBLIC POEMS

Here are two public poems performed only once at friends' funerals and never to be performed again, but I print them to show you what public duties a poet should be able to perform when asked, as we have been, to write epitaphs, elegies, epithalamia, christening songs, etc. Why should this be surprising? Get rid of the old romantic cliché of the poet being interested only in expressing his or her self.

For these important gateways to other states — life, union, death, coming of age, betrothal, society needs words arranged as well as they can be.

AN OLD ROAD FRIEND

For as long as I can remember
I have known a road called The Old Road
Which bends through and around
Railway tracks
Two Little Lakes

When you wanted to know
Why there were musk mallows
Along the roadside
Or decide
Where long ago
Vanished orchards and houses had stood
Or hear good
Stories about grandfather, father when he was young,
Rung after rung
The ladder into the past
This man could whittle
Until
At last

He has come to the bend in his road
An Old Road too
But returns soon,
How, whenever is told a story of a gravel road
Which bends through and around
Railway tracks
Two or three Little Lakes.

October 13, 1976

Young's Funeral Home, Stratford, Ontario: Wednesday, April 4, 1990
DICTA ET GESTA LAETITIAE
Sayings & Gestures of Laetitia Mae Cardwell (1915–1990)
BEING A PORTRAIT BY A FIRST COUSIN OF THE ABOVE — J.R.
~

1920   Teacher: Mae, I'm not going to strap you, but I'm going to hit the wall up in the teacher's room with the strap. Everytime I hit the wall, you cry & bawl, eh, so the other children will think I'm terrifying — which I'm not.

1926   I saw you when you were first born over at the farm. You were a naked, little red boiled-looking little thing.

1928   When our stepgrandmother Reaney had her heart attack we were visiting her in her house up on Caledonia Street. Her false teeth flew out of her mouth. I coveted her little cream pitcher, and I immediately put it up my sleeve.

1931   You never took us anywhere. How could we write an essay on what we did this summer? We never do anything around here.

1934   The gesture of throwing an embroidery hoop at her mother one snowy January morning.

1935   Summer by the clayhole pond where the raft my mother & I wanted to go out with and fish from was hopelessly beached. Mae was walking across our farm to pump water for cattle on what is now Ham Stebben's 50 acres; she picked up the raft, raised it over her head & threw it into the pond.

1937   Mother, I'm going upstairs to lie down. If anybody calls for me, tell them I'm not at home . . .

1944   On D Day there were six of us pitching a tent in the mud in Normandy.

1945   When I came home from the war I lit a fire in the parlour stove and the chimney caught fire.

1950   Dr. Fraser, you told me never to talk during an operation. What I was pointing to was the incision in the patient's stomach where you've left a pair of tweezers.

1950   I've sent you a basket of russet apples from the orchard.

1960   On phone to my mother: "Lizzie, that goose of yours with the clipped wings has flown over into our yard."

1961   Oh Tig, you're going to get it! bringing in these other dogs to eat the baby pigs.

1970   "Aren't you people ever home?" A note left on our kitchen table.

1975   Dr. Hamilton told your son just before his tonsil operation that he was a doctor of anaesthesia and was going to put him to sleep. "That's nothing," said James Stewart. "My father's a doctor of philosophy."

1976   Bring Colleen and the boys over. Billy, Brian & Gary are here and we're going to play croquet on the front lawn.

1978   This milk is sour as old Hetty.

1980   Elsie wants me to play bridge tomorrow night over at Tavistock.

1981   To my newly wed son and daughter-in-law: "That little footstool is from a chateau in Normandy. We were at a party with the officers when Jerry bombed us."

1989   I went over to Mitchell to see Helen Coveny in her coffin and it was closed. I went to see Pearl Sidwell and she was out, so I came home again. I miss the cat that used to come every day to drink some milk I'd give it. It's a wild cat somebody abandoned. Someone's kidnapped it.

1990   March 31, Saturday last. These oatmeal cookies? They're baked by me according to a recipe by Neola Makins. Have another cup of tea. What do you mean when you say that God is a Verb rather than a Noun? I've never heard anybody say that before. Sure, I'd like to read *Crazy to Kill*, Ann Cardwell. Her real name was Jean Makins. Neola remembers seeing her in Mitchell in the '20s. She was a hairdresser then. Bring it next time when you come. Goodbye. Those are my slacks out on the porch there. I'm cleaning some mud off them. Next time stay longer and tell me more about what that Indian fellow told you about God being a Verb.

I never saw Mae alive again. But in her coffin yesterday I placed a copy of her cousin's novel, as well as a twig of pussy willow and a stem of iris — two flowers that grew in the marsh on her father's farm, known as Cardwell's Flats.

◆

AVE: FAREWELL!

Good it is & wise
That after our 75-year earth walk
Our Father Heavenly
Should, He the Verbal Thrasher,
Wish to take our ripe corporeal stalk
and beat all that is dead
  Out of it,
Leaving only the alive.
Someday to be revived.

Mae, you have chosen to be consigned
To the element of fire.
Some are buried at sea.
Parsees bury their dead in the air,
But most like the earth around here.

Fire is probably what the Holy Verb
Is most like.
May your light some day reverb-
erate its candid outspoken acerb-
ic humour once more the Heaven
Within us all.

Oh mourners, rejoice & shout
Here was a fire that can never be
  Put out.

*Another thing Mae once said: Look at these family pictures in
the photo album. None of the people are touching each other.*

SEPTEMBER:
MYTHOS

Back to school, and in my youth you were liable to be hearing story poems, such as *The Rime of the Ancient Mariner*, read aloud by the teacher, Miss Helen Coveney. *Hiawatha* was a great favourite of mine; I used to drag my father's copy out into the bush, lie in a dogwood shrouded arroyo, fine quartz prisms sparkling in the dry gravel of the gulch bed, thinking about the world as a giant turtle on whose back the farm, the bush, myself, the book, all lay on a cool-clear-skied June morning not long after the Coronation of King George VI.

Years later, I found out that Longfellow got the idea for his popular epic based on Ojibway mythology from the Finnish epic *Kalevala*; in turn, the *Kalevala* was based on dozens of shaman's lays cobbled together into the story of an old Orpheus who causes the suicide of his young wife when he takes her against her will, she hating his oldness. He is continually in a struggle with the witches of North Farm, he being of South Farm — rock, icy stream, bush and chokecherry haunted, not unlike an uncle's farm up in Algoma. Either he, or a younger chap, is torn to pieces by a witch and thrown into a river in the underworld but, with a golden rake, his mother gathers the pieces up and sews him together again. In Norwesto and Noresto we have a North Farm with ravens, bears, wolves, old farmers who prophecy the weather by scanning the livers of the pigs they slaughter each fall.

What I would like to do now is show you a part of a long story poem I contemplate which uses *Kalevala* techniques on our Ontario landscape and past. Coming from the South Farm of Perth County, I also know the Thessalon area with its North Farm imagery, wild swans, cormorants, Sandhill cranes, and lonely farms. If this landscape had a voice, what would it say? Perhaps this:

I

The country we lived in was always in need of shepherds
For its ritual atonement day.
Nowadays, they use two goats, one instead of the shepherd,
The other instead of the farmsmith; they fight. He who
Loses is driven into the desert to die,
A sponge soaked with all our annual sins.
It once was that the nomad youth was stripped,

Told that if he won a fight with our smith,
Then he would become the new smith for next year.
But no one in shepherd land is taught to fight even back.
So, our smith would have to kill him, and then —
He was driven into the desert and left to die.
But, if he could trick the shepherd into fighting him?

To the west of our two great rivers with their cities
Lived the nomads in desolate areas, west of our gardens,
Our evil wheat fields. They worshipped a Voice
That spoke to them from a smouldering spice bush,
Heated to incense with the hot desert sun,
With the ecstatic effect of bridegroom, bride.
We called their Voice the Wind, and scorned it
Who sacrificed to a moon goddess who talked only
To drug-crazed women censored by officious priests.
Our gods did not like us; they sneered at our being brotoi —
Those who grew old, would soon die, unlike their perfect selves.

In retaliation, our parents hid an escaped shepherd boy
At their farm, South Farm, and they passed him off
As my brother . . . I forget, forgive me. I'll start again.

It became fashionable for those in the Big Cities
To murder shepherds. Some mad prophet
Made up a story, a dangerous story that our bridges
And temples and houses would only stand
If a shepherd's baby was enclosed alive
In their cornerstones. Hunting parties
Lumbered out into the badlands
To bring back shepherd babies for storage
In specially constructed orphanages. Others
Sacrificed them where they found them.
If the hunted children could not be captured
Or escaped, they had a price put on their heads.
Special runaway-finders trained mastiffs
To smell them out and get hold of them.
One night, a boy knocked on our door.
We had helped others from the desert;
A special convergence of stones had been left
At our gateway. My mother pretended to be pregnant.
Some years later, we brought him out of hiding,
And passed him off as my younger brother.

So far we have never found any distinguishing shepherd marks
On his body, but, then, we are not trained spotters.
Other families were doing the same as we were.
How else can you explain the sudden softening

That occurred in our country so that the priests
Realized they would have to change their stories.
Not quite so chic became human sacrifice of nomad kids.
Perhaps sacrifice everyone in a big war with Egypt?
The fact was we were tired of gods that did not love us.
Well, we dream then
Of a God who loves us so much that willingly
He would die for us as the shepherds unwillingly did.

Our parents had these problems; we had others,
For we had fallen in love with each other.
The laws against our possible union
Were cruel & wild, almost as inventively cruel
As those against shepherd boy mating with farm girl.

At night, before we turned in, we would walk
Out in the yard and look to the south
Where a few large stars blazing
Just above the southern horizon
Reminded us that, in books,
We had seen the whole of this constellation
Known as The Boat. No matter how far
The earth tipped back, we could only see half of it.
Slept in the same bed, but as we grew older,
Our parents separated us by a single canvas that was sewn
To the straw mattress and tied at the top to the rafters.
South Farm's house was small & cramped for room.

Well, we knew, that if you could sail down the river
That started in our marsh, if you kept south from its mouth,
You would eventually find another continent.
We knew the stars to sail by, and the desert island
Where the pygmy pilots lived who knew where fresh water
Springs welled up in the shallow sea-reaches
And could take us to Riff-Raff Land from whose harbour
All of The Boat would at last be seen,
As well as every criminal and misfit who had escaped our tyranny.
Behind the harbour enclave was a wilderness
Of unknown tribesmen, populus incognitus.
We thought of selling flint knives
We would make from my father's beds of chert.
That would get us bread; from driftwood we would build
Our first hut. In the Shepherd faith, we'd raise our babes,
And we'd start thinking about how to deal with the inevitable
Raid sure to come down with big ships from the Land
Between the Two Great Rivers.

II

On Saturday mornings, Ma & Pa used to go uptown
In the demi-cart. Leave us all alone to look after things.
As well as set us a task or two such as YOU scrub
The kitchen floor, and YOU clean out the pig stables.
Yes, it is years ago since the last time
I washed that kitchen floor,
And, as it started to dry, suddenly
Faces & faces & faces & faces & faces & faces & faces
Faces & faces & faces & faces & faces & faces & faces
Faces & faces & faces & faces & faces & faces & faces
Faces & faces & faces & faces & faces & faces & faces
Faces & faces & faces & faces & faces & faces & faces
Faces & faces & faces & faces & faces & faces & faces
Faces & faces & faces & faces & faces & faces & faces
Appeared all over the damp lino, the floorboards
Visible around the edges. There were whole novels & films, crowds,
Street scenes, battles, fairs, lonely vistas, insurrections.
Just then my brother came in; so he saw all this too —
Just as, pushing their way in front of everything,
We saw a stretch of road about five miles away,
Down which a big tramp and his trull, seedy charlatans,
Were trudging. Behind some bushes,
We saw them stop to attend to nature's calls,
Then change into the black suit of a minister,
She into a navy blue middy, vaguely girl guide;
They grew larger and larger, closer & closer until
They erased everyone else on the dream floor
And now we could hear them breathing
As they came nearer and nearer to South Farm. With a laugh,
I took my pail of dirty scrub water, and tossed it
. . . . OOOOOOOOOOo ooooOOOoooOOOooo
OOOOOoooooOOoooooooOOOOOO.O.O.OOOOOO. .O. o.O.o.O.o.O. o.O.o.Oo.O
Over them.
At which, gesticulating hideously with open fangs,
Hooved feet, their mouths agape with curses, they vanished.
We dried the floor with my father's wedding suit
And my mother's wedding dress, washed these,
Hung them out to dry.
On the porch we had set the table for dinner, cut bread,
Boiled potatoes, made one of those package puddings
Where you add a flavour bud half way through boiling it.

Seeing our troubled faces, they diagnosed bad tramps
Who wouldn't go away, but now — no, we could not tell them
About the dream floor and our other shared visions of things

Ahead of us in time, like the time we were running down to the pond
To swim and in the line of willows we saw a whole circus parade.
Well, next day our father came home from uptown
With tickets to that very parade and show, and it was
Just like the line of willows version only with more colour
Than shadowy wind-stirred green greys silver whites elephants,
Giraffes, tumblers, tigers in cage waggons 1234567890-=!"#$%_&'()*+
1/4@:LKJHGFDSAQWERTYUIOP?.,MNBVCXZ¢.1/2/¢.;polkmiujyhgtbvfrdcewsxazaq1!
Whenever my brother was close to me, I felt his religion
Of the Voice in the Spice Bush smoking away, entering
My body through all my orifices.

III

The servants brought in our meal.
Headcheese my mother had traded for on the market.
We hadn't touched this with our teeth,
When the tramp and the trull knocked at the door.

He was a half-uncle, a missionary, with his wife;
She an aunt-writer of children's stories, well enough
Dressed, but disturbed, cross, muddy looking,
Their eyes darting about looking for us culprits.
"As we were doing the Lord's work walking down the road
To your little spread here," they said, "a mysterious
Dirty water shower drenched us through,
Following us for a mile of wet to our skins,
Ruined a good suit and this new dress,
Soaked to the skins, unpleasant, if I may say so."
How sharply our parents asked us if we
This trick had done, but we said no
With great sincerity while feeling dread
At what the strangers might ask or do next.

And well we might. Whoever owns North Farm,
As, suddenly, they did! — has a right from an-
Cient time to any boy born on South Farm;
This, since boys are very hard to breed
On North Farm, it being virgin witch created.
Long ago my father's people used to own both farms,
But that was before things split in two
And the great Puzzletown was built between the rivers.
Such a vicious feud between North and South that my father
Dammed the river till it formed a protective marsh
Defending us from North Farm's constant encroachments.

92

Now, there was a court case, in which the guardianship
Of my brother was given to the false priest and his wife.
The day before they had the right to take him away,
Our father opened the weir so the overflow of water
Would wash our raft down to the sea after sunset,
And with six pigs as our dowry and as many casks
Of fresh water, recently handfasted in a simple ceremony,
We set out for a sky that will have at its zenith
A Great Golden Boat, south of it Golden Triangles,
Golden Squares and Hexagons, north of it Heavenly Twins
Minus their Heads, A Big Girl, her guardian a Lion
Who does not eat Lambs, a Good Giant whose club
Descends on a Tapeworm's triangular head.
We will never see these stars again because our home is here
With the pygmies, the populus incognitus, the riffraff,
The outcasts, the Golden Ark . . .

Unfinished

It's only lately that I've thought of their escaping to some other country, although I'm sure
the wicked Uncle and Aunt, who are cosmic Spiders and Antichrists of the worst type, will
show up in Riff-Raff Land to cause them trouble. I used to have a battle sequence between
North and South Farm, but it's too weird (so listeners in both Windsor and London tell me)
for release just yet. Poets are at a disadvantage right now because current events are so often
so much stranger than anything a mere poet could dream up that we're rather stymied.
However,

One lady, head of a troupe in Windsor, did ask
To see the script with an eye to a possible ballet,
And as a story, the dream floor of a magic kitchen
Which shows you things far away when it's wet
Somehow or other — makes me want to work on this some more.
                    Some Day.
For, in the beginning, was the story — and, you have to
Answer the challenge of keeping it going and also deciding
Since Alpha has been achieved just what the other letters are
In this story sentence — like where even is its Zed or its Omega?

OCTOBER:
HALLOWE'EN CONCERT

Dare you to stay overnight, they say,
Says Jack with the Lantern & Will with hair
Like mouldy hay,
Yes, stay overnight in the house by the kirkyard,
Churchyard, the way-
Side ferrywoman's hut, the house too by

Gallows Hill's blood-soiled brook,
And the auto wrecker's boneyard
Filled with rusty cars; all night long,
The big German shepherd dog barks at the shadows
In the bloodstained coupé, eternally imprinted
    Dinted
With the sudden brutal lunge & swerve across the median
    Of the truck carnivore
    With yen
    For babies in a Volkswagen
        With their careful mother.
Suddenly, at the same hour each night —
Anniversary
Of what
A driverless car breaks free from the heap,
Crashes through the gate & away
Until in the dream of the tormented child
Mr. Nothing drives it back at break of day.

Dare you to stay in the dismal yard
Of the abattoir
Where the ferocious cats live,
Bubastes & Bubastina, hell kittens,
Fed by the demented butcher
Who slavers at the beasts
He has the power of slaughter.
    Over.

Sleep in this derelict steamer
That the mad were shipped in
From Penetanguishine to Port Stanley
    Long ago
    Floating on their tears,
    Six hundred Lears
        On melted snow.
Shall I sleep on this haystack by the elm tree,
Bass roaring in the wind,
Or this strawstack by the ash tree?

———◆———

No, this empty barn through whose cracks,
This empty shed with still some hay left,
Through whose cracks the wind soprano sharps.

As the two huge, giant tramps enter,
Hoboes boister roister doister
On aqua velva and eau de quinine
Who fall to discussing ditch events
And things that happened in lonely places;
Graveyards in foggy moonlight,
Where a suave, nice, young doctor, Scottish
Digs up a pretty girl-corpse . . .

Oh but deeper that, deeper than all this
More fearsome, fff-f-f-earss-s-s-some shuddery
Deepest the hell of modern banal, empty offices
In a bankrupt stenographer glass box, sky-irritator,
Which the moneylenders have closed, to be destroyed
When?
Near Fog Wharf
The ferry blows its minor triad.
Am I the only passenger?
There's still time to avoid being born
Says an oily voice falsetto.
No one's ever survived a night on that planet.
Christ no, give me a ticket
I shall go!

MOTHER HOLLE'S SONG

Giantess!
Must
I wear these shoes of death
To walk across the bottom of yon lake
Underneath the opera house?

Have I come
Down that well
To the underground stream
That flows beneath us like a dream?

Who else can renew my cracked self
For you hold us down, rot off the dead
Parts, yea, hold us up to hold us down
And hold us down to one day hold us up
Just as my virile member is now half-past six
And now at six flourished, Christ on cross triumphant,
Next moment, Christ shrieked limp, then
From Arimathea's cave groundhogs stiff
And up to Jack in the Beanstalk heaven forever,
All this impossible without you, Mother Holle
Née Fraulein Hell, purveyor of the dark fire
Of bitter dark nothingness vacuum.

In transcribing this old hag's song
I sincerely hope I have not got it
Wrong.
Long are her teeth & sharp.
At the bottom of the well is where my parents
Tear me in half into their physiques again?
Was I dead before I was born
Or simply unborn in your underground dim garden, Frau?
Until ma and pa put together their fishing rod,
One birth canal inside another one,
Four testicles decanting in fast time/slow time
Until out of Holle's well comes back small warrior
Ready to sleep all night without dying
In the haunted house.

Oh, Holle spins a magnet hug,
Volcanoes, bones, and sour wine jug.
Lost something? She knows where it is,
Your nurse's pin, Anthony Perkins' rusty car.

Husbands, house cultivators, with their seed drills,
Draw on her lines of edibles,
Over the beds of the unborn and the un
Dead and the dead and the barely alive.
Yes, she's seedy, seedy,
A bad banker for iron which she rusty.
Good at getting down to the essential skeleton,
Helped by that lover of dead meat,
The sexton beetle,
And the Buzzard whose shadow falls on me now stinking,
In the end ready with new raiment, my own bakery and brewery —
Beer from my heart, loaves from my tenderloin?
Ugh! Such shabby resurrection.
In the female vulture's gizzard
My Flesh weaves an egg.
"Go ahead," sings Mother Holle with her big sharp teeth,
"Go ahead if you must with your schemes.
Beneath you I correct your dreams:
Some — Elijah, Jesus, Enoch, are said to've flown away
From my final exam, but — best to stay by me."
Old hellwoman, you say that when it snows
It is you plucking your geese up there?
In the sky? So, the sky is really underneath our feet?
On Christmas Eve, I put out a shoe and a stocking
For your sister Hertha
Whose stilt of smoke needs cordwainer and hosier.
Oh magic house with cellar witch and hearth fairy
And two gods sitting by the kitchen stove.
One sewing, other reading to her.

NOVEMBER:
IMAGES OF WAR & PEACE
A performance poem by James Reaney & Colleen Thibaudeau

LOST SOLDIERS

ON THE VIMY RIDGE Memorial, see the 11,285 names,
Young Canucks killed in France, graves unrecorded,
Eleven thousand and two hundred & eighty-five lost.
In alphabetical order are these names inscribed.
There are names that begin with an A.
WITH A B, with a C, a D, an E, F,G,H,I,
J,K,L,M,N,O,P,R,S — Smart, Smiley, Smillie & scores,
Scores & scores & scores & scores & scores of Smiths:
SMITH, Pte, Colin 446673. SMITH, Pte Duncan 687783, Age 19, S-
MITH, Pte E.J. 707144. SMITH, Pte Frances. SMITH, Pte G. 1737. Pte
SMITH, HAROLD Pte 7818535. SMITH, Isaac. SMITH, Lloyd. SMITH, Mat
At the end of his book on Vimy Ridge, Pierre Berton says:
"A terrible waste of human life brought on
By greedy people & tolerated too long by silent ma-
Jorities. Was it worth it? The answer, of course, is no!"
If our lives are so cheap, meaningless, let us not sing
For the State the songs of people, but instead the song —

THE SONG OF THE STYROFOAM CUP

Cross country skiing you sometimes run across
Plastic containers slick still & drifting
With the wind wing across the farms
And the frozen ponds & tarns. Along comes a styrofoam cup
Blown out from Stratford to be trapped in a chokecherry thicket
Where it keeps turning constant cir-Circular circular circular circular
With squeaky whining whang it sang:
No thing   I sing   Orphaned no friend
I have   no soul. My gods you stole
Even Santa Claus   the Easter Bunny, even the Wizard of Oz
You won't let me believe in The power you higher-ups worship
Is quite beyond my weak grasp. Yessss, send me to war,
Poison, me, evil, experimenter, Graft all my Parts onto other styrofoam cups.
How can you kill something, hurt it,
,,,,,,,,,,,,,,,,,,,,,, / /*******That
Never was allowed to be alive?

MIDNIGHT AT DOMINION SQUARE, STRATFORD

Down near the river where the War Memorial stands,
Two nude warriors in bronze togs, time-blackened,
Beaux Arts Civilization, head up, sword sheathed, head laurelled,
And Barbarism hanging his head, sackcloth on same, sword broken.
Listen to the songs of the plastic containers,
The pop cans, the styrofoam receptacles all
Sounding the whine & rattle of the dead-alive

97

Skating over the i i ice ii i i
Hark!   No, it's a dead leaf rasping, scuttling
   Murmuring smith smith sm sm sss   ith
We used to be persons, used to be s sss sss

THE RADIUM BOMB WAR

At first — World War II seemed different.
Lower casualties (consult your local war memorial)
Though 1000s of women and children . . .
But then it had a worthwhile purpose —
The defeat of a genuine evil & insane Adolf Hitler
Who appears in one of our war posters
Being treed by a Canuck Beaver who is
Furiously chewing at the tree trunk.
This at the Regional Art Gallery lately.
It's impossible to paint pictures of war.
They should be painted crazily in blood and ex-
Crement, should induce vomiting. One of the
Herb Ariss works did show this in quotation:
"Death Gully, smash, ruin, death, wreck, waste,
Mutilation, Gehenna, Sodom, Gomorrah . . ."
But World War Two really was
Civilization against Barbarity, until —
In 1945, Nagasaki was rewarded for its peaceful beauty
And its many Christians, its thousands of children,
With the second atom bomb, just after Hiroshima.
I figure that makes us worse than the broken sword guy
Soulless science won first prize for us here,
The use of Pythagoras' sacred numbers
To turn us all into styrofoam cups:

THE SONG OF THE NUCLEAR PHYSICIST

When I was little my uncle said to me:
"Come and play algebra with me.
We'll hunt the x deer through the forest of numbers."
All by myself now, I pursue God through the stars,
Made equations of energy, fought the dragon of chance,
Grown famous by it all.
Yes, at 18, I did leave the wilderness
Of numbers for a few days — I got married,
But never had any time for my two sons,
They seldom saw me, my wife not much less.
So, upset by the stillness, out of the study
I come. Wife died in her sleep. Out of my house —
There is no world left.
They! the use they made of my equations levelled it.
Horizon to horizon, the earth has become

                              One stone.

                                        James Reaney

98

THE DIEPPE GARDENS POEMS

Eugene and Peter read their poems
about Dieppe Gardens, Windsor,
a September evening, once, here in London.

Dieppe Gardens, it's not a park where I've walked,
but I remember the news of it coming — Dieppe — it came over the fences,
(field by field, farm by farm): "bad news from home."

Someone called and we would leave off hoeing,
go to the fence, and there, crying or trying not to cry,
a Windsor girl asking us to pass bad news along

though all the lists not in . . . We threw ourselves at the ground,
and that day passed, (half-hope half-fear), as if just striving
might somehow balance out the half-knowing.

A time of drought: the fine dust caked our hair; our cracked
hands, blunt fingers scrabbled to put right
a bent plant; all was more bitter-precious on that day.

Evening came; on the gravel we walked barefoot, asking,
(field by field, farm by farm), could we use the phone,
but nothing changed: only "bad news from home"

day halved slowly into night.   Your words,
Peter and Eugene, go active into memories long stilled,
and I am filled with wonder for the walkers there
                              in Dieppe Gardens now.

Colleen Thibaudeau

IMAGES OF PEACE, HUMANITY

1. The Ice Boat
               In March, there was a thaw, then it froze again.
          The whole farm was a sheet of ice streaked with sedge.
            Saturday morning, we made a clumsy ice-boat
               Out of a broken sleigh, old binder canvases.
                    The North Wind pushed us fast, fast
                    To the end of the farm all the way.

     2. Dandelions are very inexpensive musical instruments,
               Their hollow stems can play musically
                         If blown through —
                         Dandelion Horns

99

3. Maple Keys

   In June in Antler River the maple keys & the cottonwood fluff
     From that Giver,
      The cottonwood tree behind the Ceeps
        Fill the gutters and carpet the sidewalks.
                Everywhere creeps
A*1/4* inch coating of filminess drifting
     Whirling expertise of maple keys,
           Cottonwood with soft and low . . cunning . . . .

4. Jeremiah's Fields

  The gardeners & the farmers dig & hoe & sow,
They know that the ground of their plots & fields
Is the flesh of men and women, and they mix accordingly.

5. The Congress Café

Which is in Austin, Texas, a group of men & women came in,
Workers in some state office. They ordered drink then meals.
After just ten minutes, you could hear the drink they'd drunk,
Suddenly happily, speak out in them. We left at 8:30 p.m.,
But I've no doubt that the food & drink they'd taken,
Coupled some of them in matching ecstasies on Murphy beds
                     Afterwards.
            FINIS
Near the end of the year we have two festivals of the dead.
At Hallowe'en, we carve pumpkins into Jack-o'-lanterns
Which are descended from skulls the Celts put over doorways.
Next as the year darkens even more we wear smudges of blood-
Coloured cloth lest we forget the sacrifice of our young men
To the Martinet God of War. Farther on, there is a quiet time
(At the end of the year) when sometimes wonderful things happen.
Even in the trenches of the Western Front
Where one Christmas Eve the German Fritzies
Sang carols, and cigarettes, chocolates with the ene-
My they exchanged. Only in certain places, but for 24 hours
The war stopped until the officers got scared and stopped

                                  this fraternization

After all, there was still a lot of unused ammunition.
And who is responsible for this brief truce?
A Baby, a young man whose métier was healing.
 I remember the first time I saw him clearly
By the stove, my mother watering houseplants behind me,
Snow deep outside; I opened my Sunday School scrapbook
   Whose picture last Sunday given out
   Was that Raphael Madonna & Child
    Said to be painted on the lid of a barrel
      Published by Union Gospel Press,
        Mennonite Publishing House, Buffalo.

How can this Child return to help us
When we've made his Advent into shopping days before Xmas?
When we've killed his Father with banal
Misuse of the letters he gave us: ABCDEFGHIJKL
MNOPQR SMITH, Walter Pte 861281 TUVWXYZ.
With these sounds — "FIAT LUX!" — He created a universe.
With these letters, Ken & Barbie sell a million hamburgers.
When with our misuse of numbers in formulas evil & bad,
We have driven our Earth Mother mad?
We need a new ABC & new numbers,
Resistant to poison gas makers & money changers.
Quietly, as I say this, the dawn wind proclaims the day,
The stars fade, Jack with the Lantern slinks away.
Fragile as bicycle outfacing a tank,
New powers of love rise like a sun
That will make the shadows run.

James Reaney

Reprinted from "Encounter," The London Free Press, November 11, 1989

«The Book in the Tree»

DECEMBER:
SUMMA

This is a quiet time of the year
    When gates and doors are closed for a while.
Or the snow has drifted them shut.
    Big muscular howling arms of the sun known
Assssssssssssssssssssssssssssssssssssswinds!
    Scatter water turned hexagonal by frost,
OOOOOOOOOOOOOooooooo.......turned to ******
** *
Water turned solid but light as a feather,
    Over and over, to go asleep, slow down,
Hard to get arounddddddddddddddddoundddound.
    Wheels no use, only sleigh & cutter runners,
Skates, raquettes, skis — out in a blizzard just
    To see what it's like almost to snow-drown.
Vacation — take home books, but throw them
    In a corner for now, study later after Xmas.
Hurrah! Run down to the pond with the cattle
    Thirsty after me, to chop a hole in the ice
With a crowbar so they can drink. Wild, scarlet bird
    Sunset farthest south sun can get in The Goat.
Oh Aquarius, cold, clear, pure as fish, look up
    At me as I crowbar through more solid H_2O
                                  Snow
Deep on the ground, the wind blowing around more.
Help my father finish up in the stable. Gets dark
Awfully early this time of the year.
In the summer kitchen all deserted, strange,
We kick off our boots, sweep ***** off each other.
Into the winter kitchen where my mother is sprinkling
Brown sugar from a big shaker shaped like a corn cob
Into a sauce she makes out of boiling potato peelings
For poor man's pudding, old stale pieces of cake,
Magically transformed.

By the stove we sit down, he reads the newspaper
Which earlier I got from the mailbox,
Big ditch at the back, frozen, frozen,
Walk like Jesus on this winter ditch.
Xmas tree's up in parlour by piano, sacred room,
Where meetings and teas take place, quiltings & euchre,
Piano with the hydrogen down to carbon & iron of sound
Laddered on its strings. Big blue glass ball reflecting,
Plus bell made out of red rock salt, made locally,
Since no German glass during the war.
    The Xmas TB stamp this year is a snowman
    Whose hat has just been knocked off by a snowball,
    But still he smiles: I keep thinking about that . . .
    After I've finished helping my mother & father,
    I shall take out *Emily of New Moon* and read it by stove
To fall asleep eventually and feel my father's arms
    Pick me up like a sack of potatoes, deposit me in bed,
      Untying my shoes, loosening my clothing,
      Lost in sleep in the still time of the end of the year
        Guarded by Janus and Janna
      Playing cards and talking downstairs
      Till midnight strikes.
Of course, I had a dream as your day-eyes fade out and other eyes
All over your body wake up like moths & owls
& weasels & foxes & other such night walkers . . .
To dream of an orphan boy, disturbed, used to work out here,
        Ran away,
      Said he'd burn us out eventually,
      But he didn't that night.
Some years later when I met him in the navy
      He said that he had come out, but then when
    He got to the big drift by the barn
      He remembered the orange I gave him two Xmases
        Ago (in days of Yore)
   And he decided not, but went down to Kompf's south of us
    And burnt down a haystack or two.
So that all the carefully shut doors, gates, fences, the gate put up in
a tree top by Hallowe'en pranksters, carefully reconstituted by my dad as
guardians of the farm — meant nothing if a madman's loose.
    The next day we saw someone had walked through.
    The dogs knew him, so they wouldn't . . .
But I prefer another ending:
    "Guarded by Janus and Janna . . ."

After all, who taught me to give oranges to orphans?

AFTERWORD

"Your lungs are filled with us, we are the air you breathe
and you say —
Mary Donovan
       watches   The fiery furnace."

Handcuffs, Act III

These words set in lines took on new meaning and proportion this morning when spoken by twelve of Kathleen Fraser's English students who were sitting around a seminar table at the University of Western Ontario. The sound and setting were different — Patsy, David and myself spoke them together in the original production of *Handcuffs* at the Tarragon Theatre, Toronto. Oh so many years ago. Yet, despite the difference, the *feeling* was the same, a kind of exhilaration brought on by becoming one with the word together.

In November of 1989, sitting around a worn-in table, in a worn-in farmhouse, David, Kyra, Dorothy and myself read *Images of War & Peace** aloud: together, solo and chorus for one of the writers. This reading was done impromptu, at David's suggestion. Although three of us are "professional" actors, we weren't performing. We were friends/family, playing with words in lines together. That feeling was there again.

The feeling? I don't know; maybe it has something to do with breathing, thinking, speaking and being alive together. I don't know.

The words in lines in this volume offer the opportunity to explore and discover that feeling. To all of you. Gather some friends and family together and *Bon Voyage!*

Jerry Franken
March 14, 1990

**A Remembrance Day Poem*, by James Reaney and Colleen Thibaudeau